HUMANLY SPEAKING

HUMANLY SPEAKING

BY SAMUEL McCHORD CROTHERS

BOSTON AND NEW YORK

HOUGHTON MIFFLIN COMPANY

MDCCCCXII

CONTENTS

The author wishes to express his thanks to the Editors of the *Atlantic Monthly* and the *Century Magazine* for their courtesy in permitting the publication in this volume of certain essays which have appeared in their magazines.

HUMANLY SPEAKING

◆◆◆◆

HUMANLY speaking, it is impossible." So the old theologian would say when denying any escape from his own argument. His logical machine was going at full speed, and the grim engineer had no notion of putting on the brakes. His was a non-stop train and there was to be no slowing-down till he reached the terminus.

But in the middle of the track was an indubitable fact. By all the rules of argumentation it had no business to be there, trespassing on the right of way. But there it was! We trembled to think of the impending collision.

But the collision between the argument and the fact never happened. The "humanly speaking" was the switch that turned the argument safely on a parallel track, where it went whizzing by the fact without the least injury to either. Many things which are humanly speaking impossible are of the most common occurrence and the theologian knew it.

It is only by the use of this saving clause that one may safely moralize or generalize or indulge in the mildest form of prediction. Strictly speaking, no one has a right to express any opinion about such complex and incomprehensible aggregations of humanity as the United States of America or the British Empire. Humanly speaking, they both are impossible. Antecedently to experience the Constitution of Utopia as expounded by Sir Thomas More would be much more probable. It has a certain rational coherence. If it existed at all it would hang together, being made out of whole cloth. But how does the British Empire hold together? It seems to be made of shreds and patches. It is full of anomalies and temporary makeshifts. Why millions of people, who do not know each other, should be willing to die rather than to be separated from each other, is something not easily explained. Nevertheless the British Empire exists, and, through all the changes which threaten it, grows in strength.

The perils that threaten the United States of America are so obvious that anybody can see them. So far as one can see, the Republic ought to have been destroyed long ago by political corruption, race prejudice, unrestricted immigration and the growth of monopolies. The only way to account for its present existence is that there is something about it that is not so easily seen. Disease is often more easily diagnosed than health. But we should remember that the Republic is not out of danger. It is a very salutary thing to bring its perils to the attention of the too easy-going citizens. It is well to have a Jeremiah, now and then, to speak unwelcome truths.

But even Jeremiah, when he was denouncing the evils that would befall his country, had a saving clause in his gloomy predictions. All manner of evils would befall them unless they repented, and humanly speaking he was of the opinion that they couldn't repent. Said he: "Can the Ethiopian change his skin or the leopard his spots? then may ye also do good that are accustomed to do evil." Nevertheless this did not prevent him from continually exhorting them to do good, and blaming them when they didn't do it. Like all great moral teachers he acted on the assumption that there is more freedom of will than seemed theoretically possible. It was the same way with his views of national affairs. Jeremiah's reputation is that of a pessimist. Still, when the country was in the hands of Nebuchadnezzar and he was in prison for predicting it, he bought a piece of real estate which was in the hands of the enemy. He considered it a good investment. "I subscribed the deed and sealed it, and called witnesses and weighed him the money in the balances." Then he put the deeds in an earthen vessel, "that they may continue many days." For in spite of the panic that his own words had caused, he believed that the market would come up again. "Houses and vineyards shall yet be bought in this land." If I were an archæologist with a free hand, I should like to dig in that field in Anathoth in the hope of finding the earthen jar with the deed which Hanameel gave to his cousin Jeremiah, for a plot of ground that nobody else would buy.

It is the moralists and the reformers who have after all the most cheerful message for us. They are all the time threatening us, yet for our own good. They see us plunging heedlessly to destruction. They cry, "Look out!" They often do not themselves see the way out, but they have a well-founded hope that we will discover a way when our attention is called to an imminent danger. The fact that the race has survived thus far is an evidence that its instinct for self-preservation is a strong one. It has a wonderful gift for recovering after the doctors have given it up.

The saving clause is a great help to those idealists who are inclined to look unwelcome facts in the face. It enables them to retain faith in their ideals, and at the same time to hold on to their intellectual self-respect.

There are idealists of another sort who know nothing of their struggles and self-contradictions. Having formed their ideal of what ought to be, they identify it with what is. For them belief in the existence of good is equivalent to the obliteration of evil. Their world is equally good in all its parts, and is to be viewed in all its aspects with serene complacency.

Now this is very pleasant for a time, especially if one is tired and needs a complete rest. But after a while it becomes irksome, and one longs for a change, even if it should be for the worse. We are floating on a sea of beneficence, in which it is impossible for us to sink. But though one could not easily drown in the Dead Sea, one might starve. And when goodness is of too great specific gravity it is impossible to get on in it or out of it. This is disconcerting to one of an active disposition. It is comforting to be told that everything is completely good, till you reflect that that is only another way of saying that nothing can be made any better, and that there is no use for you to try.

Now the idealist of the sterner sort insists on criticizing the existing world. He refuses to call good evil or evil good. The two things are, in his judgment, quite different. He recognizes the existence of good, but he also recognizes the fact that there is not enough of it. This he looks upon as a great evil which ought to be remedied. And he is glad that he is alive at this particular juncture, in a world in which there is yet room for improvement.

Besides the ordinary Christian virtues I would recommend to any one, who would fit himself to live happily as well as efficiently, the cultivation of that auxiliary virtue or grace which Horace Walpole called " Serendipity." Walpole defined it in a letter to Sir Horace Mann : " It is a very expressive word, which, as I have nothing better to tell you, I shall endeavor to explain to you; you will understand it better by the derivation than by the definition. I once read a silly fairy tale called 'The Three Princes of Serendip.' As their Highnesses traveled, they were always making discoveries, by accidents and sagacity, of things which they were not in quest of. . . . Now do you understand *Serendipity?* " In case the reader does not understand, Walpole goes on to define "Serendipity" as "accidental sagacity (for you must know that no discovery you *are* looking for comes under this description)."

I am inclined to think that in such a world as this, where our hold on all good is precarious, a man should be on the lookout for dangers. Eternal vigilance is the price we pay for all that is worth having. But when, prepared for the worst, he goes forward, his journey will be more pleasant if he has also a "serendipitaceous" mind. He will then, by a sort of accidental sagacity, discover that what he encounters is much less formidable than what he feared. Half of his enemies turn out to be friends in disguise, and half of the other half retire at his approach. After a while such words as "impracticable" and "impossible" lose their absoluteness and become only synonyms for the relatively difficult. He has so often found a way out, where humanly speaking there was none, that he no longer looks upon a logical dilemma as a final negation of effort.

The following essays were written partly at home and partly abroad. They therefore betray the influence of some of the mass movements of the day. Any one with even a little leisure from his own personal affairs must realize that we are living in one of the most stirring times in human history. Everywhere the old order is changing. Everywhere there are confused currents both of thought and feeling.

That the old order is passing is obvious enough. That a new order is arising, and that it is on the whole beneficent, is not merely a pious hope. It is more than this: it is a matter of observation to any one with a moderate degree of "Serendipity."

IN THE HANDS OF A RECEIVER

◆◆◆◆

IT sometimes happens that a business man who is in reality solvent becomes temporarily embarrassed. His assets are greater than his liabilities, but they are not quick enough to meet the situation. The liabilities have become mutinous and bear down upon him in a threatening mob. If he had time to deal with them one by one, all would be well; but he cannot on the instant mobilize his forces.

Under such circumstances the law allows him to surrender, not to the mob, but to a friendly power which shall protect the interests of all concerned. He goes into the hands of a receiver, who will straighten out his affairs for him. I can imagine the relief which would come to one who could thus get rid, for a while, of his harassing responsibilities, and let some one else do the worrying.

In these days some of the best people I know are in this predicament in regard to their moral and social affairs. These friends of mine have this peculiarity, that they are anxious to do their duty. Now, in all generations, there have been persons who did their duty, according to their lights. But in these days it happens that a new set of lights has been turned on suddenly, and we all see more duties than we had bargained for. In the glare we see an army of creditors, each with an overdue bill in hand. Each demands immediate payment, and shakes his head when we suggest that he call again next week. We realize that our moral cash in hand is not sufficient for the crisis. If all our obligations must be met at once, there will be a panic in which most of our securities will be sacrificed.

We are accustomed to grumble over the increase in the cost of living. But the enhancement of price in the necessities of physical life is nothing compared to the increase in the cost of the higher life.

There are those now living who can remember when almost any one could have the satisfaction of being considered a good citizen and neighbor. All one had to do was to attend to one's own affairs and keep within the law. He would then be respected by all, and would deserve the most eulogistic epitaph when he came to die. By working for private profit he could have the satisfaction of knowing that all sorts of public benefits came as by-products of his activity.

But now all such satisfactions are denied. To be a good citizen you must put your mind on the job, and it is no easy one. You must be up and doing. And when you are doing one good thing there will be keen-eyed critics who will ask why you have not been doing other things which are much more important; and they will sternly demand of you, "What do you mean by such criminal negligence?"

What we call the awakening of the social conscience marks an important step in progress. But, like all progress, it involves hardship to individuals. For the higher moral classes, the saints and the reformers, it is the occasion of wholehearted rejoicing. It is just what they have, all the while, been trying to bring about. But I confess to a sympathy for the middle class, morally considered, the plain people, who feel the pinch. They have invested their little all in the old-fashioned securities, and when these are depreciated they feel that there is nothing to keep the wolf from the door. After reading a few searching articles in the magazines they feel that, so far from being excellent citizens, they are little better than enemies of society. I am not pleading for the predatory rich, but only for the well-meaning persons in moderately comfortable circumstances, whose predatoriness has been suddenly revealed to them.

Many of the most conscientious persons go about with an habitually apologetic manner. They are rapidly acquiring the evasive air of the conscious criminal. It is only a very hardened philanthropist, or an unsophisticated beginner in good works, who can look a sociologist in the eye. Most persons, when they do one thing, begin to apologize for not doing something else. They are like a one-track railroad that has been congested with traffic. They are not sure which train has the right of way, and which should go on the siding. Progress is a series of rear-end collisions.

There is little opportunity for self-satisfaction. The old-fashioned private virtues which used to be exhibited with such innocent pride as family heirlooms are now scrutinized with suspicion.

They are subjected to rigid tests to determine their value as public utilities.

Perhaps I may best illustrate the need of some receivership by drawing attention to the case of my friend the Reverend Augustus Bagster.

Bagster is not by nature a spiritual genius; he is only a modern man who is sincerely desirous of doing what is expected of him. I do not think that he is capable of inventing a duty, but he is morally impressionable, and recognizes one when it is pointed out to him. A generation ago such a man would have lived a useful and untroubled life in a round of parish duties. He would have been placidly contented with himself and his achievements. But when he came to a city pulpit he heard the Call of the Modern. The multitudinous life around him must be translated into immediate action. His conscience was not merely awakened: it soon reached a state of persistent insomnia.

When he told me that he had preached a sermon on the text, "Let him that stole steal no more," I was interested. But shortly after, he told me that he could not let go of that text. It was a live wire. He had expanded the sermon into a course on the different kinds of stealing. He found few things that did not come under the category of Theft. Spiritual goods as well as material might be stolen. If a person possessed a cheerful disposition, you should ask, "How did he get it?"

"It seems to me," I said, "that a cheerful disposition is one of the things where possession is nine tenths of the law. I don't like to think of such spiritual wealth as ill-gotten."

"I am sorry," said Bagster, "to see that your sympathies are with the privileged classes."

Several weeks ago I received a letter which revealed his state of mind:—

"I believe that you are acquainted with the Editor of the 'Atlantic Monthly.' I suppose he means well, but persons in his situation are likely to cater to mere literature. I hope that I am not uncharitable, but I have a suspicion that our poets yield sometimes to the desire to please. They are perhaps unconscious of the subtle temptation. They are not sufficiently direct and specific in their charges. I have been reading Walt Whitman's 'Song of Joys.' The subject does not attract me, but I like the way in which it is treated. There is no beating around the bush. The poet is perfectly fearless, and will not let any guilty man escape.

"' O the farmer's joys !
Ohioans, Illinoisans, Wisconsonese, Kanadians,
Iowans, Kansans, Oregonese joys.'

"That is the way one should write if he expects to get results. He should point to each individual and say, ' Thou art the man.'

"I am no poet, — though I am painfully conscious that I ought to be one, — but I have written what I call, 'The Song of Obligations.' I think it may arouse the public. In such matters we ought to unite as good citizens. You might perhaps drop a postal card, just to show where you stand."

THE SONG OF OBLIGATIONS

" O the citizen's obligations.
The obligation of every American citizen to see that every other American citizen does his duty, and to be quick about it.
The janitor's duties, the Board of Health's duties, the milkman's duties, resting upon each one of us individually with the accumulated weight of every cubic foot of vitiated air, and multiplied by the number of bacteria in every cubic centimeter of milk.

The motorman's duties, and the duty of every spry citizen not to allow himself to be run over by the motorman.

The obligation of teachers in the public schools to supply their pupils with all the aptitudes and graces formerly supposed to be the result of heredity and environment.

The duty of each teacher to consult daily a card catalogue of duties, beginning with Apperception and Adenoids and going on to Vaccination, Ventilation, and the various vivacious variations on the three R's.

The obligation resting upon the well-to-do citizen not to leave for his country place, but to remain in the city in order to give the force of his example, in his own ward, to a safe and sane Fourth of July.

The obligation resting upon every citizen to write to his Congressman.

The obligation to speak to one's neighbor who may think he is living a moral life, and who yet has never written to his Congressman.

The obligation to attend hearings at the State House.

The obligation to protest against the habit of employees at the State House of professing ignorance of the location of the committee-room where the hearings are to be held; also to protest against the habit of postponing the hearings after one has at great personal inconvenience come to the State House in order to protest.

The duty of doing your Christmas shopping early

enough in July to allow the shop-girls to enjoy their summer vacation.

The duty of knowing what you are talking about, and of talking about all the things you ought to know about.

The obligation of feeling that it is a joy and a privilege to live in a country where eternal vigilance is the price of liberty, and where even if you have the price you don't get all the liberty you pay for."

I was a little troubled over this effusion, as it seemed to indicate that Bagster had reached the limit of elasticity. A few days later I received a letter asking me to call upon him. I found him in a state of uncertainty over his own condition.

"I want you," he said, "to listen to the report my stenographer has handed me, of an address which I gave day before yesterday. I have been doing some of my most faithful work recently, going from one meeting to another and helping in every good cause. But at this meeting I had a rare sensation of freedom of utterance. I had the sense of liberation from the trammels of time and space. It was a realization of moral ubiquity. All the audiences I had been addressing seemed to flow together into one audience, and all the good causes into one good cause. Incidentally I seemed to have solved the Social Question. But now that I have the stenographic report I am not so certain."

"Read it," I said.

He began to read, but the confidence of his pulpit tone, which was one of the secrets of his power, would now and then desert him, and he would look up to me as if waiting for an encouraging "Amen."

"Your secretary, when she called me up by telephone, explained to me the object of your meeting. It is an object with which I deeply sympathize. It is Rest. You stand for the idea of poise and tranquillity of spirit. You would have a place for tranquil meditation. The thought I would bring to you this afternoon is this: We are here not to be doing, but to be.

"But of course the thought at once occurs to us, How can we *be* considering the high cost of the necessaries of life? It will be seen at once that the question is at bottom an economic one. You must have a living wage, and how can there be a living wage unless we admit the principle of collective bargaining. It is because I believe in the principle of collective bargaining that I have come here to-night to say to you working-men that I believe this strike is justifiable.

"I must leave to other speakers many interesting aspects of this subject, and confine myself to the aspect which the committee asked me to consider more in detail, namely, Juvenile Delinquency in its relation to Foreign Immigration. The relation is a real one. Statistics prove that among immigrants the proportion of the juvenile element is greater than among the native-born. This increase in juvenility gives opportunity for juvenile delinquency from which many of our American communities might otherwise be free. But is the remedy to be found in the restriction of immigration? My opinion is that the remedy is to be found only in education.

"It is our interest in education that has brought us together on this bright June morning. Your teacher tells me that this is the largest class that has ever graduated from this High School. You may well be proud. Make your education practical. Learn to concentrate, that is the secret of success. There are those who will tell you to concentrate on a single point. I would go even further. Concentrate on every point.

"I admit, as the gentleman who has preceded me has pointed out, that concentration in cities is a great evil. It is an evil that should be counteracted. As I was saying last evening to the Colonial Dames, — Washington, if he had done nothing else, would be remembered to-day as the founder of the Order of the Cincinnati. The figure of Cincinnatus at the plough appeals powerfully to American manhood. Many a time in after years Cincinnatus wished that he had never left that plough. Often amid the din of battle he heard the voice saying to him, 'Back to the Land!'

"It was the same voice I seemed to hear when I received the letter of your secretary asking me to address this grange. As I left the smoke of the city behind me and looked up at your granite hills, I said, 'Here is where they make men!' As I have been partaking of the bountiful repast prepared by the ladies of the grange, your chairman has been telling me something about this community. It is a grand community to live in. Here are no swollen fortunes; here industry, frugality, and temperance reign. These are the qualities which have given New England its great place in the councils of the nation. I know there are those who say that it is the tariff that has given it that place; but they do not know New England. There are those at this table who can remember the time when eighty-two ruddy-cheeked boys and girls trooped merrily to the little red schoolhouse under the hill. In the light of such facts as these, who can be a pessimist?

"But I must not dwell upon the past; the Boy Scouts of America prepare for the future. I am reminded that I am not at this moment addressing the Boy Scouts of America, — they come to-morrow at the same hour, — but the principle is the same. Even as the Boy Scouts of America look only at the future, so do you. We must not linger fondly on the days when cows grazed on Boston Common. The purpose of this society is to save Boston Common. That the Common has been saved many times before is true; but is that any reason why we should falter now? 'New occasions teach new duties.' Let us not be satisfied with a superficial view. While fresh loam is being scattered on the surface, commercial interests and the suburban greed to get home quick are striking at the vitals of the Common. Citizens of Boston, awake!

"Your pastor had expected to be with you this evening, but he has at the last moment discovered that he has two other engagements, each of them of long standing. He has therefore asked me to take his place in this interesting course of lectures on Church History. The subject of the lecture for the evening is — and if I am mistaken some one will please correct me — Ulphilas, or Christianity among the Goths. I cannot treat this subject from that wealth of historical information possessed by your pastor; but I can at least speak from the heart. I feel that it is well for us to turn aside from the questions of the day, for the quiet consideration of such a character as Ulphilas.

"Ulphilas seems to me to be one of those characters we ought all to know more about. I shall not weary you by discussing the theology of Ulphilas or the details of his career. It would seem more fitting that these things should be left for another occasion. I shall proceed at once to the main lesson of his life. As briefly as possible let me state the historical situation that confronted him. It is immaterial for us to inquire where the Goths were at that time, or what they were doing. It is sufficient for us to know that

the Goths at that time were pagans, mere hea-
then. Under those circumstances what did Ulphilas do? He went to the Goths. That one act re-
veals his character. If in the remaining moments
of this lecture I can enforce the lesson for us of
that one act, I shall feel that my coming here
has not been in vain.

"But some one who has followed my argument thus far may say, 'All that you have said
is true, lamentably true; but what has it to do
with the Advancement of Woman?' I answer,
it *is* the Advancement of Woman."

"How do you make that out?" I asked.

Bagster looked vaguely troubled. "There is
no such thing as an isolated moral phenomenon,"
he said, as if he were repeating something from
a former sermon; "when you attempt to remedy
one evil you find it related to a whole moral series.
But perhaps I did not make the connection plain.
My address does n't seem to be as closely rea-
soned as it did when I was delivering it. Does it
seem to you to be cogent?"

"Cogent is not precisely the word I would
use. But it seems earnest."

"Thank you," said Bagster. "I always try to

be earnest. It's hard to be earnest about so many things. I am always afraid that I may not give to all an equal emphasis."

"And now that you have stopped for a moment," I suggested, "perhaps you would be willing to skip to the last page. When I read a story I am always anxious to get to the end. I should like to know how your address comes out, — if it does come out."

Bagster turned over a dozen pages and read in a more animated manner.

"Your chairman has the reputation of making the meetings over which he presides brisk and crisp. He has given me just a minute and a half in which to tell what the country expects of this Federation of Young People. I shall not take all the time. I ask you to remember two letters — E and N. *What* does the country expect this Federation to do? E — everything. *When* does the country expect you to do it? N — now. Remember these two letters — E and N. Young people, I thank you for your attention.

"The hour is late. You, my young brother, have listened to a charge in which your urgent duties have been fearlessly declared to you. When you have performed these duties, others will be presented to you. And now, in token of our confidence in you, I give you the right hand of fellowship.

"And do you know," said Bagster, "that when I reached to give him the right hand of fellowship, he wasn't there."

We sat in silence for some time. At last he asked, hesitatingly, "What do you think of it? In your judgment is it organic or functional?"

"I do not think it is organic. I am afraid that your conscience has been over-functioning of late, and needs a rest. I know a nook in the woods of New Hampshire, under the shadow of Mount Chocorua, where you might go for six months while your affairs are in the hands of a receiver. I can't say that you would find everything satisfactory, even there. The mountain is not what it used to be. It is decadent, geologically speaking, and it suffered a good deal during the last glacial period. But you can't do much about it in six months. You might take it just as it is, — some things have to be taken that way.

"You will start to-morrow morning and begin your life of temporary irresponsibility. You will have to give up your problems for six months, but you may rest assured that they will keep. You will go by Portsmouth, where you will have ten minutes for lunch. Take that occasion for a leisurely meal. A card will be handed to you assuring you that 'The bell will ring one minute before the departure of the train. You can't get left.' Hold that thought: you can't get left; the railroad authorities say so."

"Did you ever try it," asked Bagster.

"Once," I answered.

"And did you get left?"

"Portsmouth," I said, "is a beautiful old town. I had always wanted to see it. You can see a good deal of Portsmouth in an afternoon."

The predicament in which my friend Bagster finds himself is a very common one. It is no longer true that the good die young; they become prematurely middle-aged. In these days conscience doth make neurasthenics of us all. Now it will not do to flout conscience, and by shutting our eyes to the urgencies and complexities of life purchase for ourselves a selfish calm. Neither do we like the idea of neurasthenia.

My notion is that the twentieth-century man is morally solvent, though he is temporarily embarrassed. He will find himself if he is given sufficient time. In the mean time it is well for him to consider the nature of his embarrassment. He has discovered that the world is "so full of a number of things," and he is disappointed that he is not as "happy as kings" — that is, as kings in the fairy books. Perhaps "sure enough" kings are not as happy as the fairy-book royalties, and perhaps the modern man is only experiencing the anxieties that belong to his new sovereignty over the world.

There are tribes which become confused when they try to keep in mind more than three or four numbers. It is the same kind of confusion which comes when we try to look out for more than Number One. We mean well, but we have not the facilities for doing it easily. In fact, we are not so civilized as we sometimes think.

For example, we have never carried out to its full extent the most important invention that mankind has ever made — money. Money is a device for simplifying life by providing a means of measuring our desires, and gratifying a number of them without confusion.

Money is a measure, not of commodities, but of states of mind. The man in the street expresses a profound philosophy when he says, " I feel like thirty cents." That is all that "thirty cents" means. It is a certain amount of feeling.

You see an article marked " $1.50." You pass by unmoved. The next day you see it on the bargain counter marked " 98 cents," and you say, "Come to my arms," and carry it home. You did not feel like a dollar and a half toward it, but you did feel exactly like ninety-eight cents.

It is because of this wonderful measure of value that we are able to deal with a multitude of diverse articles without mental confusion.

I am asked to stop at the department store and discover in that vast aggregation of goods a skein of silk of a specified shade, and having found it bring it safely home. Now, I am not fitted for such an adventure. Left to my own devices I should be helpless.

But the way is made easy for me. The floor-walker meets me graciously, and without chiding me for not buying the things I do not want, directs me to the one thing which would gratify my modest desire. I find myself in a little place devoted to silk thread, and with no other articles to molest me or make me afraid. The world of commodities is simplified to fit my understanding. I feel all the gratitude of the shorn lamb for the tempered wind.

At the silken shrine stands a Minerva who imparts her wisdom and guides my choice. The silk thread she tells me is equivalent to five cents. Now, I have not five cents, but only a five-dollar bill. She does not act on the principle of taking all that the traffic will bear. She sends the five-dollar bill through space, and in a minute or two she gives me the skein and four dollars and ninety-five cents, and I go out of the store a free man. I have no misgivings and no remorse because I did not buy all the things I might have bought. No one reproached me because I did not buy a four-hundred-dollar pianola. Thanks to the great invention, the transaction was complete in itself. Five cents represented one choice, and I had in my pocket ninety-nine choices which I might reserve for other occasions.

But there are some things which, as we say, money cannot buy. In all these things of the higher life we have no recognized medium of exchange. We are still in the stage of primitive barter. We must bring all our moral goods with us, and every transaction involves endless dickering. If we express an appreciation for one good thing, we are at once reproached by all the traffickers in similar articles for not taking over bodily their whole stock in trade.

For example, you have a desire for culture. You have n't the means to indulge in very much, but you would like a little. You are immediately beset by all the eager Matthew Arnolds who have heard of your desire, and they insist that you should at once devote yourself to the knowledge of the best that has been known and said in the world. All this is very fine, but you don't see how you can afford it. Is n't there a little of a cheaper quality that they could show you? Perhaps the second best would serve your purpose. At once you are covered with reproaches for your philistinism.

You had been living a rather prosaic life and would like to brighten it up with a little poetry. What you would really like would be a modest James Whitcomb Riley's worth of poetry. But the moment you express the desire the University Extension lecturer insists that what you should take is a course of lectures on Dante. No wonder that you conclude that a person in your circumstances will have to go without any poetry at all.

It is the same way with efforts at social righteousness. You find it difficult to engage in one transaction without being involved in others that you are not ready for. You are interested in a social reform that involves collective action. At once you are told that it is socialistic. You do not feel that it is any worse for that, and you are quite willing to go on. But at once your socialistic friends present you with the whole programme of their party. It is all or nothing. When it is presented in that way you are likely to become discouraged and fall back on nothing.

Now, if we had a circulating medium you would express the exact state of your desires somewhat in this way: "Here is my moral dollar. I think I will take a quarter's worth of Socialism, and twelve and a half cents' worth of old-time Republicanism, and twelve and a half cents of genuine Jeffersonian democracy, if there is any left, and a quarter's worth of miscellaneous insurgency. Let me see, I have a quarter left. Perhaps I may drop in to-morrow and see if you have anything more that I want."

The sad state of my good friend Bagster arises from the fact that he can't do one good thing without being confused by a dozen other things which are equally good. He feels that he is a miserable sinner because his moral dollar is not enough to pay the national debt.

But though we have not yet been able adequately to extend the notion of money to the affairs of the higher life, there have been those who have worked on the problem.

That was what Socrates had in mind. The Sophists talked eloquently about the Good, the True, and the Beautiful; but they dealt in these things in the bulk. They had no way of dividing them into sizable pieces for everyday use. Socrates set up in Athens as a broker in ideas. He dealt on the curb. He measured one thing in terms of another, and tried to supply a sufficient amount of change for those who were not ashamed to engage in retail trade.

Socrates draws the attention of Phædrus to the fact that when we talk of iron and silver the same objects are present to our minds, "but when any one speaks of justice and goodness, there is every sort of disagreement, and we are at odds with one another and with ourselves."

What we need to do he says is to have an idea that is big enough to include all the particular actions or facts. Then, in order to do business, we must be able to divide this so that it may serve our convenience. This is what Socrates called Philosophy.

"I am a great lover," he said, "of the processes of division and generalization; they help me to speak and think. And if I find any man who is able to see unity and plurality in nature, him I follow, and walk in his steps as if he were a god."

Even in the Forest of Arden life was not so simple as at first it seemed. The shepherd's life which "in respect of itself was a good life" was in other respects quite otherwise. Its unity seemed to break up into a confusing plurality. Honest Touchstone, in trying to reconcile the different points of view, blurted out the test question, "Hast any philosophy in thee, Shepherd?" After Bagster has communed with Chocorua for six months, I shall put that question to him.

THE CONTEMPORANEOUSNESS OF ROME

◆◆◆◆

I

YOU here, Bagster?" I exclaimed, as in the Sistine Chapel I saw an anxious face gazing down into a mirror in which were reflected the dimmed glories of the ceiling. There was an anxiety as of one who was seeking the Truth of Art at the bottom of the well.

One who is in the habit of giving unsolicited advice is likely to take for granted that his advice has been acted upon, even though experience should teach him that this is seldom the case. I had sagely counseled Bagster to go to the New Hampshire woods, in order to recuperate after his multifarious labors. I was therefore surprised to find him playing truant in Rome.

My salutation did not at first cause him to look up. He only made a mysterious sign with his hand. It was evidently a gesture which he had recently learned, and was practiced as a sort of exorcism.

"I am not going to sell you cameos or post cards," I explained.

When he recognized a familiar face, Bagster forgot all about the Last Judgment, and we were soon out-of-doors and he was telling me about himself.

"I meant to go to Chocorua as you suggested, but the congregation advised otherwise, so I came over here. It seemed the better thing to do. Up in New Hampshire you can't do much but rest, but here you can improve your taste and collect a good deal of homiletic material. So I 've settled down in Rome. I want to have time to take it all in."

"Do you begin to feel rested ?" I asked.

"Not yet. It 's harder work than I thought it would be. There 's so much to take in, and it 's all so different. I don't know how to arrange my material. What I want to do, in the first place, is to have a realizing sense of being in Rome. What 's the use of being here unless you are here in the spirit ?

"What I mean is that I should like to feel as I did when I went to Mount Vernon. It was one of those dreamy autumn days when the leaves were just turning. There was the broad Potomac, and the hospitable Virginia mansion. I had the satisfying sense that I was in the home of Washington. Everything seemed to speak of Washington. He filled the whole scene. It was a great experience. Why can't I feel that way about the great events that happened down there?"

We were by this time on the height of the Janiculum near the statue of Garibaldi. Bagster made a vague gesture toward the city that lay beneath us. There seemed to be something in the scene that worried him. "I can't make it seem real," he said. "I have continually to say to myself, 'That is Rome, Italy, and not Rome, New York.' I can't make the connection between the place and the historical personages I have read about. I can't realize that the Epistle to the Romans was written to the people who lived down there. Just back of that new building is the very spot where Romulus would have lived if he had ever existed. On those very streets Scipio Africanus walked, and Cæsar and Cicero and Paul and Marcus Aurelius, and Epictetus and Belisarius, and Hildebrand and Michelangelo, and at one time or another about every one you ever heard of. And how many people came to get emotions they could n't get anywhere else! There was Goethe. How he felt! He took it all in. And there was Shelley writing poetry in the Baths of Caracalla. And there was Gibbon."

"But we can't all expect to be Shelleys or even Gibbons," I suggested.

"I know it," said Bagster, ruefully. "But if one has only a little vessel, he ought to fill it. But somehow the historical associations crowd each other out. When I left home I bought Hare's 'Walks in Rome.' I thought I would take a walk a day as long as they lasted. It seemed a pleasant way of combining physical and intellectual exercise. But do you know, I could not keep up those walks. They were too concentrated for my constitution. I was n't equal to them. Out in California they used to make wagers with the stranger that he could n't eat a broiled quail every day for ten days. I don't see why he could n't, but it seemed that the thought of to-morrow's quail, and the feeling that it was compulsory, turned him against what otherwise might have been a pleasure. It's so with the 'Walks.' It's appalling to think that every morning you have to start out for a constitutional, and be confronted with the events of the last twenty-five centuries. The events are piled up one on another. There they are, and here you are, and what are you going to do about them?"

"I suppose that there is n't much that you can do about them," I remarked.

"But we ought to do what we can," said Bagster. "When I do have an emotion, something immediately turns up to contradict it. It 's like wandering through a big hotel, looking for your room, when you are on the wrong floor. Here you are as likely as not to find yourself in the wrong century. In Rome everything turns out, on inquiry, to be something else. There 's something impressive about a relic if it 's the relic of one thing. But if it 's the relic of a dozen different kinds of things it 's hard to pick out the appropriate emotion. I find it hard to adjust my mind to these composite associations."

"Now just look at this," he said, opening his well-thumbed Baedeker: "'Santa Maria Sopra Minerva (Pl. D. 4), erected on the ruins of Domitian's temple of Minerva, the only mediæval Gothic church in Rome. Begun A.D., 1280; was restored and repainted in 1848–55. It contains several admirable works of art, in particular Michelangelo's Christ.' "

" It 's that sort of thing that gets on my nerves. The Virgin and Minerva and Domitian and Michelangelo are all mixed together, and then everything is restored and repainted in 1848. And just round the corner from Santa Maria Sopra Minerva is the Pantheon. The inscription on the porch says that it was built by Agrippa, the son-in-law of Augustus. I try to take that in. But when I have partially done that, I learn that the building was struck by lightning and entirely rebuilt by the Emperor Hadrian.

" That information comes like the call of the conductor to change cars, just as one has comfortably settled down on the train. We must forget all about Agrippa and Augustus, and remember that this building was built by Hadrian. But it turns out that in 609 Boniface turned it into a Christian church. Which Boniface? The Pantheon was adorned with bronze columns. If you wish to see them you must go to St. Peter's, where they are a part of the high altar. So Baedeker says, but I 'm told that is n't correct either. When you go inside you see that you must let by-gones be by-gones. You are confronted with the tomb of Victor Emmanuel and set to thinking on the recent glories of the House of Savoy. Really to appreciate the Pantheon you must be well-posted in nineteenth-century history. You keep up this train of thought till you happen to stumble on the tomb of Raphael. That, of course, is what you ought to have come to see in the first place.

"When you look at the column of Trajan you naturally think of Trajan, you follow the spiral which celebrates his victories, till you come to the top of the column; and there stands St. Peter as if it were *his* monument. You meditate on the column of Marcus Aurelius, and look up and see St. Paul in the place of honor.

"I must confess that I have had difficulty about the ruins. Brick, particularly in this climate, does n't show its age. I find it hard to distinguish between a ruin and a building in the course of construction. When I got out of the station I saw a huge brick building across the street, which had been left unfinished as if the workmen had gone on strike. I learned that it was the remains of the Baths of Diocletian. Opening a door I found myself in a huge church, which had a long history I ought to have known something about, but did n't.

" Now read this, and try to take it in : ' Returning to the Cancelleria, we proceed to the Piazza Campo de' Fiori, where the vegetable market is held in the morning, and where criminals were formerly executed. The bronze statue of the philosopher Giordano Bruno, who was burned here as a heretic in 1600, was erected in 1889. To the east once lay the Theatre of Pompey. Behind it lay the Porticus of Pompey where Cæsar was murdered, B.C. 44.'

" It economizes space to have the vegetable market and the martyrdom of Giordano Bruno and the assassination of Julius Cæsar all close together. But they are too close. The imagination has n't room to turn round. Especially as the market-women are very much alive and cannot conceive that any one would come into the Piazza unless he intended to buy vegetables. Somehow the great events you have read about don't seem to have impressed themselves on the neighborhood. At any rate, you are conscious that you are the only person in the Piazza Campo de' Fiori who is thinking about Giordano Bruno or Julius Cæsar; while the price of vegetables is as intensely interesting as it was in the year 1600 A.D. or in 44 B.C.

"How am I to get things in their right perspective? When I left home I had a pretty clear and connected idea of history. There was a logical sequence. One period followed another. But in these walks in Rome the sequence is destroyed. History seems more like geology than like logic, and the strata have all been broken up by innumerable convulsions of nature. The Middle Ages were not eight or ten centuries ago; they are round the next block. A walk from the Quirinal to the Vatican takes you from the twentieth century to the twelfth. And one seems as much alive as the other. You may go from schools where you have the last word in modern education, to the Holy Stairs at the Lateran, where you will see the pilgrims mounting on their knees as if Luther and his protest had never happened. Or you can, in five minutes, walk from the Renaissance period to 400 B.C.

"When I was in the theological seminary I had a very clear idea of the difference between Pagan

Rome and Christian Rome. When Constantine came, Christianity was established. It was a wonderful change and made everything different. But when you stroll across from the Arch of Titus to the Arch of Constantine you wonder what the difference was. The two things look so much alike. And in the Vatican that huge painting of the triumph of Constantine over Maxentius does n't throw much light on the subject. Suppose the pagan Maxentius had triumphed over Constantine, what difference would it have made in the picture?

"They say that seeing is believing, but here you see so many things that are different from what you have always believed. The Past does n't seem to be in the past, but in the present. There is an air of contemporaneousness about everything. Do you remember that story of Jules Verne about a voyage to the moon? When the voyagers got a certain distance from the earth they could n't any longer drop things out of the balloon. The articles they threw out did n't fall down. There was n't any down; everything was round about. Everything they had cast out followed them. That 's the way Rome makes you feel about history. That which happened a thousand years ago is going on still. You can't get rid of it. The Roman Republic is a live issue, and so is the Roman Empire, and so is the Papacy.

"The other day they found a ruined Arch of Marcus Aurelius in Tripoli, and began to restore it. New Italy is delighted at this confirmation of its claims to sovereignty in North Africa. The newspapers treat Marcus Aurelius as only a forerunner of Giolitti. By the way, I never heard of Giolitti till I came over here. But it seems that he is a very great man. But when ancient and modern history are mixed up it's hard to do any clear thinking. And when you do get a clear thought you find out that it is n't true. You know Dr. Johnson said something to the effect that that man is little to be envied whose patriotism would not gain force upon the plain of Marathon, or whose feelings would not grow warmer among the ruins of Rome. Marathon is a simple proposition. But when one is asked to warm his enthusiasm by means of the Roman monuments, he naturally asks, 'Enthusiasm over what?' Of course, I don't mean to give up. I'm faint though pursuing. But I'm afraid that Rome is not a good place to rest in."

"I'm afraid not," I said, "if you insist on keeping on thinking. It is not a good place in which to rest your mind."

II

I think Bagster is not the first person who has found intellectual difficulty here. Rome exists for the confusion of the sentimental traveler. Other cities deal tenderly with our preconceived ideas of them. There is one simple impression made upon the mind. Once out of the railway station and in a gondola, and we can dream our dream of Venice undisturbed. There is no doge at present, but if there were one we should know where to place him. The city still furnishes the proper setting for his magnificence. And London with all its vastness has, at first sight, a familiar seeming. The broad and simple outlines of English history make it easy to reconceive the past.

But Rome is disconcerting. The actual refuses to make terms with the ideal. It is a vast storehouse of historical material, but the imagination

is baffled in the attempt to put the material together.

When Scott was in Rome his friend "advised
him to wait to see the procession of Corpus
Domini, and hear the Pope

> Saying the high, high mass
> All on St. Peter's day.

He smiled and said that these things were more
poetical in the description than in reality, and
that it was all the better for him not to have seen
it before he wrote about it."

Sir Walter's instinct was a true one. Rome
is not favorable to historical romance. Its atmosphere is eminently realistic. The historical romancer is flying through time as the air-men fly
through space. But the air-men complain that
they sometimes come upon what they call "air
holes." The atmosphere seems suddenly to give
way under them. In Rome the element of Time
on which the imagination has been flying seems
to lose its usual density. We drop through a
Time-hole, and find ourselves in an inglorious
anachronism.

I am not sure that Bagster has had a more
difficult time than his predecessors, who have at-

tempted to assort their historical material. For in the days before historical criticism was invented, the history of Rome was very luxuriant. "Seeing Rome" was a strenuous undertaking, if one tried to be intelligent.

There was an admirable little guide-book published in the twelfth century called "Mirabilia Urbis Romæ." One can imagine the old-time tourist with this mediæval Baedeker in hand, issuing forth, resolved to see Rome in three days. At the end of the first day his courage would ooze away as he realized the extent of his ignorance. With a hurried look at the guide-book and a glance at the varied assortment of ruins, he would try to get his bearings. All the worthies of sacred and profane history would be passing by in swift procession.

"After the sons of Noah built the tower of confusion, Noah with all his sons came to Italy. And not far from the place where Rome now is they founded a city in his name, where he brought his travail and life to an end." To come to the city of Noah was worth a long journey. Just think of actually standing on the spot where Shem, Ham, and Japhet soothed the declining years of their father! It was hard to realize it all. And it appears that Japhet, always an enterprising person, built a city of his own on the Palatine Hill. There is the Palatine, somewhat cluttered up with modern buildings of the Cæsars, but essentially, in its outlines, as Japhet saw it.

But there were other pioneers to be remembered. "Saturn, being shamefully entreated by his son Jupiter," founded a city on the Capitoline Hill. One wonders what Shem, Ham, and Japhet thought of this, and whether their sympathies were with Jupiter who was seeking to get a place in the sun.

It is hard to understand the complicated politics of the day. At any rate, a short time after, Hercules came with a band of Argives and established a rival civic centre. In the meantime, Janus had become mixed up with Roman history and was working manfully for the New Italy. On very much the same spot "Tibris, King of the Aborigines" built a city, which must be carefully distinguished from those before mentioned.

All this happened before Romulus appeared upon the scene. One with a clear and comprehensive understanding of this early history might enjoy his first morning's walk in Rome. But to the middle-aged pilgrim from the West Riding of Yorkshire, who had come to Rome merely to see the tomb of St. Peter, it was exhausting.

But perhaps mediæval tradition did not form a more confusing atmosphere than the sentimental admiration of a later day. In the early part of the nineteenth century a writer begins a book on Rome in this fashion: "I have ventured to hope that this work may be a guide to those who visit this wonderful city, which boasts at once the noblest remains of antiquity, and the most fault-less works of art; which possesses more claims to interest than any other city; which has in every age stood foremost in the world; which has been the light of the earth in ages past, the guiding star through the long night of ignorance, the fountain of civilization to the whole Western world, and which every nation reverences as the common nurse, preceptor, and parent."

This notion of Rome as the venerable parent of civilization, to be approached with tenderly reverential feelings, was easier to hold a hundred years ago than it is to-day. There was nothing to contradict it. One might muse on "the grandeur

that was Rome," among picturesque ruins covered
with flowering weeds. But now a Rome that is
obtrusively modern claims attention. And it is
not merely that the modern world is here, but
that our view of antiquity is modernized. We
see it, not through the mists of time, but as a
contemporary might.

When Ferrero published his history we were
startled by his realistic treatment. It was as if
we were reading a newspaper and following the
course of current events. Cæsar and Pompey
and Cicero were treated as if they were New
York politicians. Where we had expected to
see stately figures in togas we were made to see
hustling real-estate speculators, and millionaires,
and labor leaders, and ward politicians, who were
working for the prosperity of the city and, incidentally, for themselves. It was all very different
from our notions of classic times which we had
imbibed from our Latin lessons in school. But it
is the impression which Rome itself makes upon
the mind.

One afternoon, among the vast ruins of Hadrian's Villa, I tried to picture the villa as it was
when its first owner walked among the buildings

which his whim had created. The moment Hadrian himself appeared upon the scene, antiquity seemed an illusion. How ultra-modern he was, this man whom his contemporaries called "a searcher out of strange things"! These ruins could not by the mere process of time become venerable, for they were in their very nature novelties. They were the playthings of a very rich man. There they lie upon the ground like so many broken toys. They are just such things as an enormously rich man would make to-day if he had originality enough to think of them. Why should not Hadrian have a Vale of Tempe and a Greek theatre and a Valley of Canopus, and ever so many other things which he had seen in his travels, reproduced on his estate near Tivoli?

An historian of the Empire says: "The character of Hadrian was in the highest degree complex, and this presents to the student a series of apparently unreconciled contrasts which have proved so hard for many modern historians to resolve. A thorough soldier and yet the inaugurator of a peace policy, a 'Greekling' as his Roman subjects called him, and saturated with Hellenic ideas, and yet a lover of Roman antiquity; a poet and an artist, but with a passion for business and finance; a voluptuary determined to drain the cup of human experience and, at the same time, a ruler who labored strenuously for the well-being of his subjects; such were a few of the diverse parts which Hadrian played."

It is evident that the difficulty with the historians who find these unreconciled contrasts is that they try to treat Hadrian as an "ancient" rather than as a modern. The enormously rich men who are at present most in the public eye present the same contradictions. Hadrian was a thorough man of the world. There was nothing venerable about him, though much that was interesting and admirable.

Now what a man of the world is to a simple character like a saint or a hero, that Rome has been to cities of the simpler sort. It has been a city of the world. It has been cosmopolitan. "Urbs et orbis" suggests the historic fact. The fortunes of the city have become inextricably involved in the fortunes of the world.

A part of the confusion of the traveler comes from the fact that the Roman city and the Roman world are not clearly distinguished one from the other. The New Testament writer distinguishes between Jerusalem as a geographical fact and Jerusalem as a spiritual ideal. There has been, he says, a Jerusalem that belongs to the Jews, but there is also Jerusalem which belongs to humanity, which is free, which is "the mother of us all."

So there has been a local Rome with its local history. And there has been the greater Rome that has impressed itself on the imagination of the world. Since the destruction of Carthage the meaning of the word "Roman" has been largely allegorical. It has stood for the successive ideas of earthly power and spiritual authority.

Rome absorbed the glory of deeds done elsewhere. Battles were fought in far-off Asia and Africa. But the battlefield did not become the historic spot. The victor must bring his captives to Rome for his triumph. Here the pomp of war could be seen, on a carefully arranged stage, and before admiring thousands. It was the triumph rather than the battle that was remembered. All the interest culminated at this dramatic moment. Rome thus became, not the place where history was made, but the place where it was celebrated. Here the trumpets of fame perpetually sounded.

This process continued after the Empire of the Cæsars passed away. The continuity of Roman history has been psychological. Humanity has "held a thought." Rome became a fixed idea. It exerted an hypnotic influence over the barbarians who had overcome all else. The Holy Roman Empire was a creation of the Germanic imagination, and yet it was a real power. Many a hardheaded Teutonic monarch crossed the Alps at the head of his army to demand a higher sanction for his own rule of force. When he got himself crowned in the turbulent city on the Tiber he felt that something very important had happened. Just how important it was he did not fully realize till he was back among his own people and saw how much impressed they were by his new dignities.

Hans Christian Andersen begins one of his stories with the assertion, " You must know that the Emperor of China is a Chinaman and that all whom he has about him are Chinamen also." The assertion is so logical in form that we are inclined to accept it without question. Then we remember that in Hans Christian Andersen's day, and for a long time before, the Emperor of China was not a Chinaman and the great grievance was that Chinamen were the very people he would not have about him.

When we speak of the Roman Catholic Church, we jump at the conclusion that it is the church of the Romans and that the people of Rome have had the most to do with its extension. This theory has nothing to recommend it but its extreme verbal simplicity. As a matter of fact, Rome has never been noted for its pious zeal. Such warmth as it has had has been imparted to it by the faithful who have been drawn from other lands; as, according to some theorists, the sun's heat is kept up by a continuous shower of meteors falling into it.

To-day, the Roman Church is more conscious of its strength in Massachusetts than it is near the Vatican. At the period when the Papacy was at its height, and kings and emperors trembled before it in England and in Germany, the Popes had a precarious hold on their own city. Rome was a religious capital rather than a religious centre. It did not originate new movements. Missionaries of the faith have not gone forth from it, as they went from Ireland. It is not in Rome that we find the places where the saints received their spiritual illuminations, and fought the good fight, and gathered their disciples. Rome was the place to which they came for judgment, as Paul did when he appealed to Cæsar. Here heretics were condemned, and here saints, long dead, were canonized. Neither the doctrines nor the institutions of the Catholic Church originated here. Rome was the mint, not the mine. That which received the Roman stamp passed current throughout the world.

In the political struggle for the New Italy, Rome had the same symbolic character. Mazzini was never so eloquent as when portraying the glories of the free Rome that was to be recognized, indeed, as the mother of us all. The Eternal City, he believed, was to be the regenerating influence, not only for Europe but for all the world. All the romantic enthusiasm of Garibaldi flamed forth at the sight of Rome. All other triumphs signified nothing till Rome was the acknowledged capital of Italy. Silently and steadily Cavour worked toward the same end. And at last Rome gathered to herself the glory of the heroes who were not her own children.

If we recognize the symbolic and representative character of Roman history, we can begin to understand the reason for the bewilderment which comes to the traveler who attempts to realize it in imagination. Roman history is not, like the tariff, a local issue. The most important events in that history did not occur here at all, though they were here commemorated. So it happens that every nation finds here its own, and reinforces its traditions. In the Middle Ages, the Jewish traveler, Benjamin of Tudela, found much to interest him. In Rome were to be found two brazen pillars of Solomon's Temple, and there was a crypt where Titus hid the holy vessels taken from Jerusalem. There was also a statue of Samson and another of Absalom.

The worthy Benjamin doubtless felt the same thrill that I did when looking up at the ceiling of the Church of Santa Maria Maggiore. I was told that it was gilded with the first gold brought from America. The statement, that the church was founded on this spot because of a vision that came to Pope Liberius in the year 305 A.D., left

me unmoved. It was of course a long time ago;
but then, I had no mental associations with Pope
Liberius, and there was no encyclopædia at hand
in which I might look him up. Besides, "the
church was reërected by Sixtus III in the year
432, and was much altered in the twelfth century."
But the gold on the ceiling was a different matter. That was romantically historical. It came
from America in the heroic age. I thought of the
Spanish galleons that brought it over, and of
Columbus and Cortés and Alvarado. After that,
to go into the Church of Santa Maria Maggiore
was like taking a trip to Mexico.

In the course of my daily walks, I passed the
Church of Santa Pudenziana, said to be the
oldest in Rome, and recently modernized. It is
on the spot where Pudens, the host of St. Peter,
is said to have lived with his daughters Praxedis
and Pudentiana. This is interesting, but the
English-speaking traveler is likely to pass by
Pudentiana's church, and seek out the church of
her sister St. Praxed. And this not for the sake
of St. Praxed or her father Pudens or even of his
guest St. Peter, but for the sake of a certain English poet who had visited the church once.

Close to the Porta San Paolo is the great tomb of the Roman magnate, Gaius Cestius, which was built before the birth of Christ. One can hardly miss seeing it, because it is near one of the most sacred pilgrimage places of Rome, the grave of John Keats.

Each traveler makes his own Rome; and the memories which he takes away are the memories which he brought with him.

III

As for my friend Bagster, now that he has come to Rome, I hope he may stay long enough to allow it to produce a more tranquilizing effect upon him. When he gives up the attempt to take it all in by an intellectual and moral effort, he may, as the saying is, "relax."

There is no other place in which one may so readily learn the meaning of that misused word "urbanity." Urbanity is the state of mind adapted to a city, as rusticity is adapted to the country. In each case the perfection of the adaptation is evidenced by a certain ease of manner in the presence of the environment. There is an absence of fret and worry over what is involved in the situation. A countryman does not fret over dust or mud; he knows that they are forms of the good earth out of which he makes his living. He may grumble at the weather, but he is not surprised at it, and he is ready to make the best of it.

This adaptation to nature is easy for us, for we are rustics by inheritance. Our ancestors lived in the open, and kept their flocks and were mighty hunters long before towns were ever thought of. So when we go into the woods in the spring, our self-consciousness leaves us and we speedily make ourselves at home. We take things for granted, and are not careful about trifles. A great many things are going on, but the multiplicity does not distract us. We do not need to understand.

For we have primal sympathies which are very good substitutes for intelligence. We do not worry because nature does not get on faster with her work. When we go out on the hills on a spring morning, as our forbears did ten thousand years ago, it does not fret us to consider that things are going on very much as they did then. The sap is mounting in the trees; the wild flowers are pushing out of the sod; the free citizens of the woods are pursuing their vocations without regard to our moralities. A great deal is going on, but nothing has come to a dramatic culmination.

Our innate rusticity makes us accept all this in the spirit in which it is offered to us. It is nature's way and we like it, because we are used to it. We take what is set before us and ask no questions. It is spring. We do not stop to inquire as to whether this spring is an improvement on last spring or on the spring of the year 400 B.C. There is a timelessness about our enjoyment. We are not thinking of events set in a chronological order, but of a process which loses nothing by reason of repetition.

Our attitude toward a city is usually quite different. We are not at our ease. We are querulous and anxious, and our interest takes a feverish turn. For the cities of our Western world are new-fangled contrivances which we are not used to, and we are worried as we try to find out whether they will work. These aggregations of humanity have not existed long enough to seem to belong to the nature of things. It is exciting to be invited to "see Seattle grow," but the exhibition does not yield a "harvest of a quiet eye." If Seattle should cease to grow while we are looking at it, what should we do then?

But with Rome it is different. Here is a city which has been so long in existence that we look upon it as a part of nature. It is not accidental or artificial. Nothing can happen to it but what has happened already. It has been burned with fire, it has been ravaged by the sword, it has been ruined by luxury, it has been pillaged by barbarians and left for dead. And here it is to-day the scene of eager life. Pagans, Christians, reformers, priests, artists, soldiers, honest workmen, idlers, philosophers, saints, were here centuries ago. They are here to-day. They have continuously opposed each other, and yet no species has been exterminated. Their combined activities make the city.

When one comes to feel the stirring of primal sympathies for the manifold life of the city, as he does for the manifold life of the woods, Rome ceases to be distracting. The old city is like the mountain which has withstood the hurts of time, and remains for us, "the grand affirmer of the present tense."

THE AMERICAN TEMPERAMENT

◆◆◆◆

I

STOPPING at some selected spot on the mountain road, the stage-driver will direct the stranger's attention to a projecting mass of rock which bears some resemblance to a human countenance. There is the "Old Man of the Mountains," or the "Old Woman," as the case may be.

If the stranger be of a docile disposition he will see what he is told to see. But he will be content with the vague suggestion and will not push the analogy too far. The similitude is strictly confined to the locality. It is enough if from a single point the mountain seems almost human. From any other point it will seem to be merely mountainous.

A similar caution is necessary in regard to the resemblances between a nation and an individual. When we talk of a national character or temperament, we are using an interesting and bold figure of speech. We speak of millions of people as if they were one. Of course, a nation is not one kind of person; it is composed of many kinds of persons. These persons are diverse in character. All Scotchmen are not canny, nor all Irishmen happy-go-lucky. Those who know a great many Chinamen are acquainted with those who are idealists with little taste for plodding industry. It is only the outsider who is greatly impressed by the family resemblance. To the more analytic mind of the parent each child is, in a most remarkable degree, different from the others.

When we take such typical characters as John Bull and Brother Jonathan as representing actual Englishmen or Americans, we put ourselves in the way of contradiction. They are not good likenesses. An English writer says: "As the English, a particularly quick-witted race, tinged with the colors of romance, have long cherished a false pride in their reputed stolidity, and have accepted with pleasant equanimity the figure of John Bull as their national signboard, though he does not resemble them, so Americans plume themselves on the thought that they are dying of nervous energy."

There is much truth in this. One may stand at Charing Cross and watch the hurrying crowds and only now and then catch sight of any one who suggests the burly John Bull of tradition. The type is not a common one, at least among city dwellers.

But when we attribute a temperament to a nation, we do not necessarily mean that all the people are alike. We only mean that there are certain ways of thinking and feeling that are common to those who have had the same general experience. The national temperament is manifested not so much in what the people are as in what they admire and instinctively appreciate.

Let us accept the statement that the English are a quick-witted and romantic people who have accepted with pleasant equanimity the reputation for being quite otherwise. Why should they do this? Why should they take pride in their reputed stolidity rather than in their actual cleverness. Here is a temperamental peculiarity that is worth looking into.

John Bull may be a myth, but Englishmen have been the mythmakers. They have for generations delighted in picturing him. He represents a combination of qualities which they admire. Dogged, unimaginative, well-meaning, honest, full of whimsical prejudices, and full of common sense, he is loved and honored by those who are much more brilliant than he.

John Bull is not a composite photograph of the inhabitants of the British Isles. He is not an average man. He is a totem. When an Indian tribe chooses a fox or a bear as a totem, they must not be taken too literally. But the symbol has a real meaning. It indicates that there are some qualities in these animals that they admire. They have proved valuable in the tribal struggle for existence.

Those who belong to the cult of John Bull take him as the symbol of that which has been most vital and successful in the island story. England has had more than its share of men of genius. It has had its artists, its wits, its men of quick imagination. But these have not been the builders of the Empire, or those who have sustained it in the hours of greatest need. Men of a slower temper, more solid than brilliant, have been the nation's main dependence. "It's dogged as does it." On many a hard-fought field men of the bull-dog breed have with unflinching tenacity held their own. In times of revolution they have maintained order, and never yielded to a threat. Had they been more sensitive they would have failed. Their foibles have been easily forgiven and their virtues have been gratefully recognized.

When we try to form an idea of that which is most distinctive in the American temperament, we need not inquire what Americans actually are. The answer to that question would be a generalization as wide as humanity. They are of all kinds. Among the ninety-odd millions of human beings inhabiting the territory of the United States are representatives of all the nations of the Old World, and they bring with them their ancestral traits.

But we may ask, When these diverse peoples come together on common ground, what sort of man do they choose as their symbol? There is a typical character understood and appreciated by all. In every caricature of Uncle Sam or Brother Jonathan we can detect the lineaments of the American frontiersman.

James Russell Lowell, gentleman and scholar

that he was, describes a type of man unknown to the Old World: —

> " This brown-fisted rough, this shirt-sleeved Cid,
> This backwoods Charlemagne of Empires new.
> Who meeting Cæsar's self would slap his back,
> Call him ' Old Horse ' and challenge to a drink."

Mr. Lowell bore no resemblance to this brown-fisted rough. He would not have slapped Cæsar on the back, and he would have resented being himself greeted in such an unconventional fashion. Nevertheless he was an American and was able to understand that a man might be capable of such improprieties and at the same time be a pillar of the State. It tickled his fancy to think of a fellow citizen meeting the imperial Roman on terms of hearty equality.

> " My lungs draw braver air, my breast dilates
> With ampler manhood, and I face both worlds."

Dickens, with all his boisterous humor and democratic sympathies, could not interpret Jefferson Brick and Lafayette Kettle and the other expansive patriots whom he met on his travels. Their virtues were as a sealed book to him. Their boastful familiarity was simply odious.

To understand Lowell's exhilaration one must

enter into the spirit of American history. It has been the history of what has been done by strong men who owed nothing to the refinements of civilization. The interesting events have taken place not at the centre, but on the circumference of the country. The centrifugal force has always been the strongest. There has been no capital to which ambitious youths went up to seek their fortune. In each generation they have gone to the frontier where opportunities awaited them. There they encountered, on the rough edges of society, rough-and-ready men in whom they recognized their natural superiors. These men, rude of speech and of manner, were resourceful, bold, far-seeing. They were conscious of their power. They were laying the foundations of cities and of states and they knew it. They were as boastful as Homeric heroes, and for the same reason. There was in them a rude virility that found expression in word as well as in deed.

Davy Crockett, coon-hunter, Indian fighter, and Congressman, was a great man in his day. It does not detract from his worth that he was well aware of the fact. There was no false modesty about this backwoods Charlemagne. He wrote of himself, "If General Jackson, Black Hawk, and me were to travel through the United States we would bring out, no matter what kind of weather, more people to see us than any other three people now living among the fifteen millions now inhabiting the United States. And what would it be for? As I am one of the persons mentioned I would not press the question further. What I am driving at is this. When a man rises from a low degree to a place he ain't used to, such a man starts the curiosity of the world to know how he got along."

Davy Crockett understood the temper of his fellow citizens. A man who rises by his own exertions from a low position to "a place he ain't used to" is not only an object of curiosity, but he elicits enthusiastic admiration. Any awkwardness which he exhibits in the position which he has achieved is overlooked. We are anxious to know how he got along.

Every country has its self-made men, but usually they are made to feel very uncomfortable. They are accounted intruders in circles reserved for the choicer few. But in America they are assured of a sympathetic audience when they tell of the way they have risen in the world. There is no need for them to apologize for any lack of early advantages, for they are living in a self-made country. We are in the habit of giving the place of honor to the beginner rather than to the continuer. For the finisher the time is not ripe.

II

The most vivid impressions of Americans have always been anticipatory. They have felt themselves borne along by a resistless current, and that current has, on the whole, been flowing in the right direction. They have never been confronted with ruins that tell that the land they inhabit has seen better days. Yesterday is vague; To-day may be uncertain; To-morrow is alluring; and the Day after to-morrow is altogether glorious. George Herbert pictured religion as standing on tiptoe waiting to pass to the American strand. Not only religion but every other good thing has assumed that attitude of expectant curiosity.

Even Cotton Mather could not avoid a tone of pious boastfulness when he narrated the doings of New England. Everything was remarkable. New England had the most remarkable providences, the most remarkable painful preachers,

the most remarkable heresies, the most remarkable witches. Even the local devils were in his
judgment more enterprising than those of the old
country. They had to be in order to be a match
for the New England saints.

The staid Judge Sewall, after a study of the
prophecies, was of the opinion that America was
the only country in which they could be adequately fulfilled. Here was a field large enough
for those future battles between good and evil
which enthralled the Puritan imagination. To be
sure, it would be said, there is n't much just now
to attract the historian whose mind dwells exclu-
sively on the past. But to one who dips into the
future it is thrilling. Here is the battlefield of
Armageddon. Some day we shall see "the spirits
of devils working miracles, which go forth unto
the kings of the earth, and of the whole world, to
gather them to the battle of that great day of
God Almighty." Just *when* that might take place
might be uncertain but *where* it would take place
was to them more obvious.

In the days of small things the settlers in the
wilderness had large thoughts. They felt themselves to be historical characters, as indeed they

were. They were impressed by the magnitude of the country and by the importance of their relation to it. Their language took on a cosmic breadth.

Ethan Allen could not have assumed a more masterful tone if he had had an Empire at his back instead of undisciplined bands of Green Mountain Boys. Writing to the Continental Congress, he declares that unless the demands of Vermont are complied with " we will retire into the fastnesses of our Green Mountains and will wage eternal warfare against Hell, the Devil, and Human Nature in general." And Ethan Allen meant it.

The love of the superlative is deeply seated in the American mind. It is based on no very careful survey of the existing world. It is a conclusion to which it is easy to jump. I remember one week, traveling through the Mississippi Valley, stopping every night in some town that had something which was advertised as the biggest in the world. On Friday I reached a sleepy little village which seemed the picture of contented mediocrity. Here, thought I, I shall find no bigness to molest me or make me afraid. But when I sat down to write a letter on the hotel stationery I was confronted with the statement, " This is the biggest little hotel in the State."

When one starts a tune it is safer to start it rather low, so as not to come to grief on the upper notes. In discussing the American temperament it is better to start modestly. Instead of asking what excellent qualities we find in ourselves, we should ask what do other nations most dislike in us. We can then have room to rise to better things. There is a family resemblance between the worst and the best of any national group. Kipling, in his lines " To an American," may set the tune for us. It is not too high. His American is boastful, careless, and irrationally optimistic.

> " Enslaved, illogical, elate,
>   He greets the embarrassed gods, nor fears
> To shake the iron hand of Fate
>   Or match with Destiny for beers."

A person who would offer to shake hands with Fate is certainly lacking in a fine sense of propriety. His belief in equality makes him indifferent to the note of distinction. " He dubs his dreary brethren kings." Of course they are not kings, but that makes no difference. It makes little difference whether anything corresponds to the name he chooses to give to it. For there is

> " A cynic devil in his blood
> That bids him mock his hurrying soul."

This impression of a mingling of optimism, cynicism, and hurry is one which is often made upon those who are suddenly plunged into American society. In any company of Americans who are discussing public affairs the stranger is struck by what seems the lack of logical connection between the statements of facts and the judgments passed upon them. The facts may be most distressing and yet nobody seems much distressed, still less is any one depressed. The city government is in the hands of grafters, the police force is corrupt, the prices of the necessaries of life are extortionate, the laws on the statute book are not enforced, and new laws are about to be enacted that are foolish in the extreme. Vast numbers of undesirable aliens are coming into the country and bringing with them ideas that are opposed to the fundamental principles of the republic. All this is told with an air of illogical elation. The conversation is interspersed with anecdotes of the exploits of good-natured rascals. These are received with smiles or tolerant laughter. Every one seems to have perfect confidence that the country is a grand and glorious place to live in, and that all will come out well in the end.

Is this an evidence of a cynic humor in the blood, or is it a manifestation of childish optimism? Let us frankly answer that it may be one or the other or both. There are cynics and sentimentalists who are the despair of all who are seriously working for better citizenship. But the chances are that the men to whom our stranger was listening were neither cynics nor sentimentalists, but idealists who had the American temperament.

Among those who laughed good-naturedly over the temporary success of the clever rascal may have been those who had been giving their energies to the work of prevention of just such misdeeds. They are reformers with a shrewd twinkle in their eyes. They take a keen intellectual pleasure in their work, and are ready to give credit to any natural talent in their antagonist. If they are inclined to take a cheerful view of the whole situation it is because they are in the habit of looking at the situation as a whole. The predomi-

nance of force is actually on their side and they
see no reason to doubt the final result. They have
learned the meaning of the text, "Fret not thyself
because of evildoers." In fact the evildoer may
not have done so much harm as one might think.
Nor is he really such a hopeless character. There
is good stuff in him, and he yet may be used for
many good purposes. They laugh best who laugh
last, and their good-natured laughter was anticipatory. There are forces working for righteousness
which they have experienced. On the whole
things are moving in the right direction and they
can afford to be cheerful.

This is the kind of experience which comes to
those who are habitually dealing with crude materials rather than with finished products. They
cannot afford to be fastidious; they learn to take
things as they come and make the best of them.
The doctrine that things are not as they seem
is a cheerful one, to a person who is accustomed
to dealing with things which turn out to be
better than at first they seemed. The unknown
takes on a friendly guise and awakens a pleasant
curiosity. That is the experience of generations
of pioneers and prospectors. They have found a

continent full of resources awaiting men of courage and industry. The opportunities were there; all that was needed was the ability to recognize them when they appeared in disguise.

III

And the human problem has been the same as the material one. Europe has sent to America not the finished products of her schools and her courts, but millions of people for whom she had no room. They were in the rough; they had to be made over into a new kind of citizen. This material has often been of the most unpromising appearance. It has often seemed to superficial observers that little could be made of it. But the attempt has been made. And those who have worked with it, putting skill and patience into their work, have been agreeably surprised. They have come to see the highest possibilities in the commonest lumps of clay.

The satisfaction that is taken in the common man is not in what he is at the present moment, but in what he has shown himself capable of becoming. Give him a chance and all the graces may be his. The American idealist admits that many of his fellow citizens may be rather dreary brethren, but so were many of the kings of whom nothing is remembered but their names and dates. Only now and then is one seen who is every inch a king. But such a person is a proof of what may be accomplished. It may take a long time for the rank and file to catch up with their leaders. But where the few are to-day the many will be to-morrow; for they are all travelling the same road.

The visitor in the United States, especially if he has spent his time in the great cities of the East, may go away with the idea that democracy is a spent force. He will see great inequalities in wealth and position. He will be struck by the fact that autocratic powers are wielded which would not be tolerated in many countries of Europe. He will notice that it is very difficult to give direct expression to the will of the people.

But he will make a mistake if he attributes these things to the growth of an aristocratic senti-ment. They are a part of an evolution that is thoroughly democratic. The distinctive thing in an aristocracy is not the fact that certain people enjoy privileges. It lies in the fact that these privileged people form a class that is looked upon as superior. An aristocratic class must not only take itself seriously; it must be taken seriously by others.

In America there are groups of persons more successful than the average. They are objects of curiosity, and, if they are well-behaved, of respect. Their comings and goings are chronicled in the newspapers, and their names are familiar. But it does not occur to the average man that they are anything more than fortunate persons who emerged from the crowd, and who by and by may be lost in the crowd again. What they have done, others may do when their time comes. The inequalities are inequalities of circumstance and not of nature.

The commonplace American follows unworthy leaders and has admiration for cheap success. But he cherishes no illusions in regard to the objects of his admiration. They have done what he would like to do, and what he hopes to be able to do sometime. He thinks of the successful men as being of the same kind with himself. They are more fortunate, that is all.

IV

The same temperamental quality is seen in the American idealist. His attitude toward his spiritual leaders is seldom that of meek discipleship. It is rather that of frank, outspoken comradeship. No mysterious barrier separates the great man from the common man. One has more, the other has less, that is all.

The men who have cherished the finest ideals have insisted that these should be shared by the multitude. In a newspaper of sixty years ago there is this contemporary character sketch: "Ralph Waldo Emerson is the most erratic and capricious man in America. He is emphatically a democrat of the world, and believes that what Plato thought, another man may think. What Shakespeare sang, another man may know as well. As for emperors, kings, queens, princes, or presidents, he looks upon them as children in masquerade. He has no patience with the chicken-hearted who refer to mouldy records or old almanacs to ascertain if they may say that their souls are their own. Mr. Emerson is a strange compound of contradictions. Always right in practice, and sometimes in theory. He is a sociable, accessible, republican sort of man, and a great admirer of nature."

Could any better description be given of the kind of man whom Americans delight to honor? This "sociable, accessible, republican sort of man" happened to be endowed with gifts denied in such full measure to his countrymen. But they were gifts which they understood and appreciated. He was one of them, and expressed and interpreted their habitual thought. Luther used to declare that no one who had never had trials and temptations could understand the Holy Scriptures. And one might say that no one who had never taken part in a town meeting, or listened to the talk of neighbors at the country store, or traveled in an "accommodation train" in the Middle West, can fully understand Emerson.

Critics have often written of the optimism of Emerson as if he were one of those who did not perceive the darker side of things. Nothing could be more untrue to his temper of mind. Emerson was cheerful, but he never pretended that the world was an altogether cheerful place to live in.

Indeed, it distinctly needed cheering up, and that, according to him, is what we are here for.

It might be possible to make out a list of matters of fact treated by Emerson and his friend Carlyle. They would be essentially the same. When it came to hard facts, one was as unflinching in his recognition as the other. There was nothing smug in Emerson's philosophy. He never took an apologetic attitude nor attempted to minimize difficulties. There was no attempt to justify the ways of God to man. But while agreeing in regard to the facts the friends differed as to their conclusions. In reading Carlyle one seems to stand at the end of a world struggle that has proved unavailing. Everything has been tried, and everything has failed. Alas! Alas!

Emerson sees the same facts, but he seems to be standing at the beginning. The moral world is still without form and void, but the creative spirit is brooding upon it. "Sweet is the genesis of things." Emerson is pleased with the world, not because he thinks its present condition is very good, but because he sees so much room for it to become better. It is a most promising experiment. It furnishes an abundance of the raw materials of righteousness.

Nor does he flatter himself that the task of betterment is an easy one, or that the end is in sight. It is not a world where wishes, even good wishes, are fulfilled without effort. There are inexorable laws not of our making. The whims of good people are not respected.

> "For Destiny never swerves
>   Nor yields to man the helm."

The struggle is stern and unrelenting. It taxes all our energies. And yet it is exhilarating. There is a moral quick-wittedness which sees the smile behind the threatening mask of Fate. Destiny is after all a good comrade for the brave and the self-reliant.

> "He forbids to despair,
>   His cheeks mantle with mirth,
> And the unimagined good of man
>   Is yeaning at the birth."

The riddle of existence is seen not from the Old World point of view, but from that of the new. It is of the nature of a surprise. The Sphinx of Emerson is not carved in stone. It is not silent and motionless, waiting for answers that do not come.

It is the American Sphinx leading in a game of hide-and-seek. The mystery of existence baffles us, not because there is no answer, but because there are so many. They are infinite in number, and all of them are true. They wait for the mind large enough to harbor them in all their variety, and serene enough not to be annoyed because their contradictions are not at once reconciled.

The catalogue of ills may be never so long, but it fails to depress one who sees everything in the making.

> " I heard a poet answer
>   Aloud and cheerfully,
>   ' Say on, sweet Sphinx! thy dirges
>   Are pleasant songs to me.'
>
>   .   .   .   .   .
>
> " Uprose the merry Sphinx,
>   And crouched no more in stone ;
>   She melted into purple cloud,
>   She silvered in the moon."

This conception of the merry Sphinx may seem strange to the dyspeptic philosopher pondering on the inscrutableness of the universe. But the prospectors in the mining camps of the Far West, and the builders of new cities understand what Emerson meant. Their experience of the ups and downs of fortune has taught them how to find pleasure in uncertainty. You never can tell how anything will turn out till you try. That's the fun of it. They are quite ready to believe that the same thing holds good in the higher life.

Or take the lines on "Worship." How can Worship be personified? Emerson's picture is not that of a patriarch on bended knee; it is that of a vigorous youth picking himself up after he has been knocked down by his antagonist.

> "This is he, who, felled by foes,
>   Sprung harmless up, refreshed by blows."

Religion is a kind of spiritual resilience. It is that which makes a man come back with new vigor to his work after his first failure. It is the ability to make a new beginning.

In Emerson the American hurry is transformed into something of spiritual significance. A new commandment is given to the good man — Be quick! Keep moving!

> "Trenchant Time behoves to hurry,
>
>   .   .   .   .   .   .
>
> O wise man, hearest thou the least part,
> Seest thou the rushing metamorphosis,
>
> Dissolving all that fixture is,
> Melts things that be to things that seem."

Morality and religion must be speeded up if they are to do any useful work in this swift world.

If the ideals of the saints and reformers were criticized, so were those of the scholars. Matthew Arnold's definition of culture was that of a man of books. It was the knowledge of the best that had been said and known in the past. Emerson's lines entitled " Culture " begin with a characteristic question and end with an equally characteristic affirmation. The question is —

> " Can rules or tutors educate
> The semigod whom we await ? "

The affirmation is that the man of culture is one who

> " to his native centre fast,
> Shall into Future fuse the Past,
> And the world's flowing fates in his own mould recast."

According to this definition Abraham Lincoln, with his slight knowledge of the best things of the past, but with the power to fuse such knowledge as he had and to recast it in his own mould, was a man of culture. And all true Americans would agree with him.

Emerson, like the "sociable, accessible, republican sort of man" that he was, was the foe of special privilege. The best things were, in his judgment, the property of all. He would take religion from the custody of the priests, and culture from the hands of schoolmasters, and restore them to their proper place, among the inalienable rights of man. They were simply forms of the pursuit of happiness of which the Declaration of Independence speaks. It is a right of which no potentates can justly deprive the citizen.

Above all, he would protest against everything which tends to deprive any one of the happiness of the forward look. There was a cheerful confidence that the great forces are on our side. Now and then the clouds gather and obscure the vision, but:

> " There are open hours
> When God's will sallies free
> And the dull idiot may see
> The flowing fortunes of a thousand years. "

This is the American doctrine of "Manifest Destiny" spiritually discerned.

V

But one need not go so far back as Emerson to see the higher reaches of the American temperament. Perhaps in no one have they been revealed with more distinctness than in William James. There are those who consider it dispraise of a philosopher to suggest that his work has local color. However that may be, William James thought as an American as certainly as Plato thought as a Greek. His way of philosophizing was one that belonged to the land of his birth.

He was as distinctly American as was Daniel Boone. Daniel Boone was no renegade taking to the woods that he might relapse into savagery. He was a civilized man who preferred to be the maker of civilization rather than to be its victim. He preferred to blaze his own way through the forest. When he saw the smoke of a neighbor's chimney it was time for him to move on. So William James was led by instinct from the crowded highways to the dim border-lands of human experience. He preferred to dwell in the debatable lands. With a quizzical smile he listened to the dignitaries of philosophy. He found their completed systems too stuffy. He loved the wildernesses of thought where shy wild things hide — half hopes, half realities. They are not quite true now, — but they may be by and by.

As other men are interested in the actual, so he was interested in the possible. The possibilities are not so highly finished as the facts that have been proved, but there are a great many more of them, and they are much more important. There are more things in the unexplored forest than in the clearing at its edge. Truth to him was not a field with metes and bounds. It was a continent awaiting settlement. First the bold pathfinders must adventure into it. Its vast spaces were infinitely inviting, its undeveloped resources were alluring. And not only did the path-finder interest him but the path-loser as well. But for his heedless audacity the work of exploration would languish. Was ever a philosopher so humorously tender to the intellectual vagabonds, the waifs and strays of the spiritual world!

Their reports of vague meanderings in the border-land were listened to without scorn. They might be ever so absent-minded and yet have stumbled upon something which wiser men had missed. No one was more keen to criticize the hard-and-fast dogmas of the wise and prudent or more willing to learn what might, by chance, have been revealed unto babes. The one thing he demanded was space. His universe must not be finished or inclosed. After a rational system had been formulated and declared to be the Whole, his first instinct was to get away from it. He was sure that there must be more outside than there was inside. "The 'through-and-through' universe seems to suffocate me with its infallible, impeccable all-pervasiveness. Its necessity with no possibilities, its relations with no subjects, make me feel as if I had entered into a contract with no reserved rights."

Formal philosophy seemed to him to be "too buttoned-up and white-chokered and clean-shaven a thing to speak for the vast, slow-breathing, unconscious Kosmos with its dread abysses and its unknown tides. The freedom we want is not the freedom, with a string tied to its leg and warranted not to fly away, of that philosophy. Let it fly away, we say, from *us*. What then?"

To this American there must be a true democracy among the faculties of the mind. The logical understanding must not be allowed to put on priggish airs. The feelings have their rights also. "They may be as prophetic and as anticipatory of truth as anything else we have." There must be give and take; "what hope is there of squaring and settling opinions unless Absolutism will hold parley on this common ground and admit that all philosophies are hypotheses, to which all our faculties, emotional as well as logical, help us, and the truest of which will in the final integration of things be found in possession of the men whose faculties on the whole had the best divining power?"

Do not those words give us a glimpse of the American mind in its natural working. Its genius is anticipatory. It is searching for a common ground on which all may meet. It puts its trust not in the thinker who can put his thoughts in the most neat form, but the man whose faculties have *on the whole the best divining power*.

To listen to William James was to experience an illogical elation — and to feel justified in it. He was an unsparing critic of things as they are, but his criticism left us in no mood of depression. Our interest is with things as they are going to be. The universe is growing. Let us grow with it.

THE UNACCUSTOMED EARS OF EUROPE

❖❖❖❖

I

WHEN, as a child, I learned the Westminster Catechism by heart I found the Ten Commandments easy to remember. There was something straightforward in these prohibitions. Once started in the right direction one could hardly stray from the path. But I stumbled over the question, in regard to certain Commandments, "What are the reasons annexed?"

That a commandment should be committed to memory seemed just. I was prepared to submit to the severest tests of verbal accuracy. But that there should be "reasons annexed," and that these also should be remembered, seemed to my youthful understanding a grievance. It made the path of the obedient hard. To this day there is a haziness about the "reasons" that contrasts with the sharp outlines of the commandments.

I fancy that news-gatherers have the same experience. They are diligent in collecting items of news and reporting them to the world, but it is a real hardship to them to have to give any rational account of these bits of fact. They tell what is done in different parts of the world, but they forget to mention "the moving why they did it." The consequence is that, in this age of instantaneous communication, we know what is going on in other countries, but it seems very irrational. The rational elements have been lost in the process of transmission.

There has, for example, been no lack of news cabled across the Atlantic in regard to the nominations for President of the United States. The European reader is made aware that a great deal of strong feeling has been evoked, and strong language used. When a picturesque term of reproach has been hurled by one candidate at another it is promptly reported to a waiting world. But the "reasons annexed" are calmly ignored. The consequence is that the reader is confirmed in his exaggerated idea of the nervous irritability of the American people. There seems to be a periodicity in their seizures. At intervals of four years they indulge in an orgy of mutual recrimination, and then suddenly return to their normal state of money-getting. It is all very unaccountable. Doubtless the most charitable explanation is the climate.

It was after giving prominence to an unusually vivid bit of political vituperation that a conservative London newspaper remarked, " All this is characteristically American, but it shocks the unaccustomed ears of Europe."

As I read the rebuke I felt positively ashamed of my country and its untutored ways. I pictured Europe as a dignified lady of mature years listening to the screams issuing from her neighbor's nursery. She had not been used to hearing naughty words called out in such a loud tone of voice. Instead of discussing their grievances calmly, they were actually calling one another names.

It was therefore with a feeling of chastened humility that I turned to the columns devoted to the more decorous doings of Europe. Here I should find examples worthy of consideration. They are drawn from the homes of ancient civility. Would that our rude politicians might be brought under these refining influences and learn how to behave!

But alas! When we drop in upon our neighbors, unannounced, things are sometimes not so tidy as they are on the days "at home." The hostess is flustered and evidently has troubles of her own. So, as ill-luck would have it, it is with Dame Europe's household. The visitor from across the Atlantic is surprised at the obstreperousness of the more vigorous members of the family. Evidently a great many interesting things are going on, but the standard of deportment is not high.

While the unaccustomed ears of Europe were shocked at the shrill cries from the rival conventions at Chicago and Baltimore, there was equal turbulence in the Italian Parliament at Rome. There were shouts and catcalls and every sign of uncontrollable violence. What are the "reasons annexed" to all this uproar? I do not know. In Budapest such unparliamentary expressions as "swine," "liar," "thief," and "assassin" were freely used in debate. An honorable member who had been expelled for the use of too strong language, returned to "shoot up" the House.

The chairman, after dodging three shots, declared that he must positively insist on better order.

In the German Reichstag a member threatens the Kaiser with the fate of Charles the First, if he does not speedily mend his ways. He suggests as a fit Imperial residence the castle where the Mad King of Bavaria was allowed to exercise his erratic energies without injury to the commonweal. At the mention of Charles the First the chamber was in an uproar, and amid a tumult of angry voices the session was brought to a close.

In Russia, unseemly clamor is kept from the carefully guarded ears of the Czar. There art conspires with nature to produce peace. We read of the Czar's recent visit to his ancient capital: "The police during the previous night made three thousand arrests. The Czar and Czarina drove through the city amid the ringing of bells, and with banners flying."

On reading this item the American reader plucks up heart. If, during the Chicago convention, the police had made three thousand arrests the sessions might have been as quiet as those of the Duma.

Even the proceedings of the British House of Commons are disappointing to the pilgrim in search of decorum. The Mother of Parliaments has trouble with her unruly brood.

We enter the sacred precincts as a Member rises to a point of order.

"I desire to ask your ruling, Mr. Speaker, as to whether the honorable gentleman is entitled to allude to Members of the House as miscreants."

The Speaker: "I do not think the term 'miscreant' is a proper Parliamentary expression."

This is very elementary teaching, but it appears that Mr. Speaker is not infrequently compelled to repeat his lesson. It is "line upon line and precept upon precept."

The records of the doings of the House contain episodes which would be considered exciting in Arizona. We read: "For five minutes the Honorable George Lansbury defied the Speaker, insulted the Prime Minister, and scorned the House of Commons. He raved in an ecstasy of passion; challenging, taunting, and defying." The trouble began with a statement of Mr. Asquith's. "Then up jumped Mr. Lansbury, his face contorted with passion, and his powerful rasping voice dominating the whole House. Shouting and waving his arms, he approached the Government Front Bench with a curious crouching gait, like a boxer leaving his corner in the ring. One or two Liberals on the bench behind Mr. Asquith half rose, but the Prime Minister sat stolidly gazing above the heads of the opposition, his arms folded, and his lips pursed. Mr. Lansbury had worked himself up into a state of frenzy and, facing the Prime Minister, he shouted, 'You are beneath my contempt! Call yourself a gentleman! You ought to be driven from public life.'"

I cannot remember any scene like this in Disraeli's novels. The House of Commons used to be called the best club in Europe. But that, says the Conservative critic, was before the members were paid.

II

But certain changes, like the increased cost of living, are going on everywhere. The fact seems to be that all over the civilized world there is a noticeable falling-off in good manners in public discussion. It is useless for one country to point the finger of scorn at another, or to assume an air of injured politeness. It is more conducive to good understanding to join in a general confession of sin. We are all miserable offenders, and there is little to choose between us. The conventionalities which bind society together are like the patent glue we see advertised on the streets. A plate has been broken and then joined together. The strength of the adhesive substance is shown by the way it holds up a stone of considerable weight attached to it. The plate thus mended holds together admirably till it is put in hot water.

I have no doubt but that a conservative Chinese gentleman would tell you that since the Republic came in there has been a sad falling-off in the observance of the rules of propriety as laid down by Confucius. The Conservative newspapers of England bewail the fact that there has been a lamentable change since the present Government came in. The arch offender is "that political Mahdi, Lloyd George, whose false prophecies have made deluded dervishes of hosts of British workmen, and who has corrupted the manners of Parliament itself."

This wicked Mahdi, by his appeals to the passions of the populace, has destroyed the old English reverence for Law.

I do not know what may be the cause, but the American visitor does notice that the English attitude towards the laws of the realm is not so devout as he had been led to expect. We have from our earliest youth been taught to believe that the law-abidingness of the Englishman was innate and impeccable. It was not that, like the good man of whom the Psalmist speaks, he meditated on the law day and night. He did n't need to. Decent respect for the law was in his blood. He simply could not help conforming to it.

And this impression is confirmed by the things which the tourist goes to see. The stately mansions embowered in green and guarded by immemorial oaks are accepted as symbolic of an ordered life. The multitudinous rooks suggest security which comes from triumphant legality. No irresponsible person shoots them. When one enters a cathedral close he feels that he is in a land that frowns on the crudity of change. Here everything is a "thousand years the same." And how decent is the demeanor of a verger!

When the pilgrim from Kansas arrives at an ancient English inn he feels that he must be on his good behavior. Boots in his green apron is a lesson to him. He is not like a Western hotel bell-boy on the way to becoming something else. He knows his place. Everybody, he imagines, in this country knows his place, and there is no unseemly crowding and pushing. And what stronger proof can there be that this is a land where law is reverenced than the demeanor of a London policeman. There is no truculence about him, no show of physical force. He is so mild-eyed and soft of speech that one feels that he has been shielded from rude contact with the world. He represents the Law in a land where law is sacred. He is instinctively obeyed. He has but to wave his hand and traffic stops.

When the traveler is told that in the vicinity of the House of Commons traffic is stopped to allow a Member to cross the street, his admiration increases. Fancy a Congressman being treated with such respect! But the argument which, on the whole, makes the deepest impression is the deferential manners of the tradesmen with their habit of saying, "Thank you," apropos of

nothing at all. It seems an indication of perpetual gratitude over the fact that things are as
they are.

But when one comes to listen to the talk of the
day one is surprised to find a surprising lack of
docility. I doubt whether the Englishman has
the veneration for the abstract idea of Law which
is common among Americans. Indeed, he is accustomed to treat most abstractions with scant
courtesy. There is nothing quite corresponding
to the average American's feeling about a decision of the Supreme Court. The Law has spoken,
let all the land keep silent. It seems like treason
to criticize it, like anarchy to defy it.

Tennyson's words about "reverence for the laws
ourselves have made" needs to be interpreted by
English history. It is a peculiar kind of reverence
and has many limitations. A good deal depends
on what is meant by "ourselves." An act of Parliament does not at once become an object of
reverence by the members of the opposition
party. It was not, they feel, made by *them*, it was
made by a Government which was violently opposed to them and which was bent on ruining
the country.

It is only after a sufficient time has elapsed to allow for the partisan origin to be forgotten, and for it to become assimilated to the habits of thought and manner of life of the people that it is deeply respected. The English reverence is not for statute law, but for the common law which is the slow accretion of ages. A new enactment is treated like the new boy at school. He must submit to a period of severe hazing before he is given a place of any honor.

To the American when an act of Congress has been declared constitutional, a decent respect for the opinion of mankind seems to suggest that verbal criticism should cease. The council of perfection is that the law should be obeyed till such time as it can be repealed or explained away. If it should become a dead letter, propriety would demand that no evil should be spoken of it. Since the days of Andrew Jackson the word "nullification" has had an ugly and dangerous sound.

But to the Englishman this attitude seems somewhat superstitious. The period of opposition to a measure is not ended when it has passed Parliament and received the royal assent. The question is whether it will receive the assent of the people. Can it get itself obeyed? If it can, then its future is assured for many generations. But it must pass through an exciting period of probation.

If it is a matter that arouses much feeling the British way is for some one to disobey and take the consequences. Passive resistance — with such active measures as may make the life of the enforcers of the law a burden to them — is a recognized method of political and religious propagandism.

In periods when the national life has run most swiftly this kind of resistance to what has been considered the tyranny of lawmakers has always been notable. Emerson's "the chambers of the great are jails" was literally true of the England of the seventeenth century. Every one who made any pretension to moral leadership was intent on going to jail in behalf of some principle or another.

John Bunyan goes to jail rather than attend the parish church, George Fox goes to jail rather than take off his hat in the presence of the magistrate. Why should he do so when there was no Scripture for it ? When it was said that the Scripture had nothing to say about hats, he was ready with his triumphant reference to Daniel III, 21, where it is said that the three Hebrew children wore "their coats, their hosen, their hats and their other garments" in the fiery furnace. If Shadrach, Meshach, and Abed-nego wore their hats before Nebuchadnezzar and kept them on even in the fiery furnace, why should a free-born Englishman take his hat off in the presence of a petty Justice of the Peace ? Fervent Fifth Monarchy men were willing to die rather than acknowledge any king but King Jesus who was about to come to reign. Non-juring bishops were willing to go to jail rather than submit to the judgment of Parliament as to who should be king in England. Puritans and Covenanters of the more logical sort refused to accept toleration unless it were offered on their own terms. They had been a "persecuted remnant" and they proposed to remain such or know the reason why.

Beneath his crust of conformity the Briton has an admiration for these recalcitrant individuals who will neither bow the knee to Baal nor to his betters. He likes a man who is a law unto himself. Though he has little enthusiasm for the abstract "rights of man," he is a great believer in "the liberty of prophesying." The prophet is not without honor, even while he is being stoned.

Just at this time things are moving almost as rapidly as they did in the seventeenth century. There is the same clash of opinion and violence of party spirit. All sorts of non-conformities struggle for a hearing. One is reminded of that most stirring period, which is so delightful to read about, and which must have been so trying for quiet people to live through.

A host of earnest and wide-awake persons are engaged in the task of doing what they are told not to do. Their enthusiasm takes the form of resistance to some statute made or proposed.

The conscientious women who throw stones through shop windows, and lay violent hands on cabinet ministers, do so, avowedly, to bring certain laws into disrepute. They go on hunger-strikes, not in order to be released from prison, but in order to be treated as political prisoners. They insist that their methods should be recognized as acts of legitimate warfare. They may be extreme in their actions, but they are not alone in their theory.

The Insurance Law, by which all workers whose wages are below a certain sum are compulsorily insured against sickness and the losses that follow it, is just going into effect. Its provisions are necessarily complicated, and its administration must at first be difficult. The Insurance-Law Resisters are organized to nullify the act. Its enormities are held up before all eyes, and it is flouted in every possible way. According to this law, a lady is compelled to pay three-pence a week toward the insurance fund for each servant in her employ. Will she pay that three-pence? No! Though twenty acts of Parliament should declare that it must be done, she will resist. As for keeping accounts, and putting stamps in a book, she will do nothing of the kind. What is it about a stamp act that arouses such fierceness of resistance?

High-born ladies declare that they would rather go to jail than obey such a law. At a meeting at Albert Hall the Resisters were addressed by a duchess who was " supported by a man-servant." What can a mere Act of Parliament do when confronted by such a combination as that? Passive resistance takes on heroic proportions when a duchess and a man-servant confront the Law with haughty immobility.

In the mean time, Mr. Tom Mann goes to jail, amid the applause of organized labor, for advising the British soldier not to obey orders when he is commanded to fire on British workingmen.

Mr. Tom Mann is a labor agitator, while Mr. Bonar Law is the leader of the Conservative party; but when it comes to legislation which he does not like, Mr. Bonar Law's language is fully as incendiary. He is not content with opposing the Irish Home Rule Bill: he gives notice that when it has become a law the opposition will be continued in a more serious form. The passage of the bill, he declares, will be the signal for civil war. Ulster will fight. Parliament may pass the Home Rule Bill, but when it does so its troubles will have just begun. Where will it find the troops to coerce the province?

One of the most distinguished Unionist Members of Parliament, addressing a great meeting at Belfast says, " You are sometimes asked whether you propose to resist the English army? I reply that even if this Government had the wickedness (which, on the whole, I believe), it is wholly lacking in the nerve required to give an order which in my deliberate judgment would shatter for years the civilization of these islands." If the Government does not have the nerve to employ its troops, "It will be for the moon-lighters and the cattle-maimers to conquer Ulster themselves, and it will be for you to show whether you are worse men, or your enemies better men, than the forefathers of you both. But I note with satisfaction that you are preparing yourselves by the practice of exercises, and by the submission to discipline, for the struggle which is not unlikely to test your determination. The Nationalists are determined to rule you. You are determined not to be ruled. A collision of wills so sharp may well defy the resources of a peaceful solution. . . . On this we are agreed, that the crisis has called into existence one of those supreme issues of conscience amid which the ordinary landmarks of permissible resistance to technical law are submerged."

When one goes to the Church to escape from

these sharp antagonisms, he is confronted with huge placards giving notice of meetings to protest against " The Robbery of God." The robber in this case is the Government, which proposes to disendow, as well as disestablish, the Church in Wales. Noble lords denounce the outrage. Mr. Lloyd George replies by reminding their lordships that their landed estates were, before the dissolution of the monasteries under Henry VIII, Church property. If they wish to make restitution of the spoil which their ancestors took, well and good. But let them not talk about the robbery of God, while their hands are " dripping with the fat of sacrilege."

The retort is effective, but it does not make Mr. Lloyd George beloved by the people to whom it is addressed. Twitting on facts has always been considered unmannerly.

III

When we hear the acrimonious discussions and the threats of violence, it is well to consider the reason for it all. I think the reason is one that is not discreditable to those concerned. These are not ordinary times, and they are not to be judged by ordinary standards. England is at the present time passing through a revolution, the issues of which are still in doubt. Revolutionary passions have been liberated by the rapid course of events. "Every battle of the warrior is with confused noise." The confused noise may be disagreeable to persons of sensitive nerves, but it is a part of the situation.

When we consider the nature of the changes that have been made in the last few years, and the magnitude of those which are proposed, we do not wonder at the tone of exasperation which is common to all parties.

It is seldom that a constitutional change, like that which deprived the House of Lords of powers exercised for a thousand years, has been made without an appeal to arms. But there was no civil war. Perhaps the old fashion of sturdy blows would have been less trying to the temper.

A revolution is at the best an unmannerly proceeding. It cannot be carried on politely, because it involves not so much a change of ideas and methods as a change of masters. A change of ideas may be discussed in an amiable and orderly way. The honorable gentlemen who have the responsibility for the decision are respectfully asked to revise their opinions in the light of new evidence which, by their leave, will be presented.

But a change of masters cannot be managed so inoffensively. The honorable gentlemen are not asked to revise their opinions. They are told that their opinions are no longer important. The matter is severely personal. The statement is not, "We do not believe in your ideas"; it is, "We do not believe in *you*."

When political discussion takes this turn, then there is an end to the amenities suited to a more quiet time. It is no longer a question as to which is the better cause, but as to which is the better man.

Mr. Asquith, who has retained in this revolutionary period the manners of the old school, recently said in his reply to a delegation of his opponents, "When people are on opposite sides of a chasm they may be courteous to one another, and regret the impossibility of their shaking hands, or doing more than wave a courteous gesture across so wide a space."

These are the words of a gentleman in politics, and express a beautiful ideal. But they hardly describe the present situation. As to waving a courteous salutation to the people on the other side, — that depends on who the people are. If you know them and have been long familiar with their good qualities, the courteous salutation is natural. They are, as you know, much better than their opinions.

But it is different when they are people whom you do not know, and with whom you have nothing in common. You suspect their motives, and feel a contempt for their abilities. They are not of your set. The word "gentleman" is derived from the word *gens*. People of the same *gens* learn to treat each other in a considerate way. Even when they differ they remember what is due to gentle blood and gentle training.

It is quite evident that the challenge of the new democracy to the old ruling classes has everywhere produced exasperation. It is no longer easy to wave courteous salutations across the chasms which divide parties. Political discussion takes a rude turn. It is no longer possible to preserve the proprieties. We may expect the minor moralities to suffer while the major moralities are being determined by hard knocks.

Good manners depend on the tacit understanding of all parties as to their relations to one another. Nothing can be more brutal than for one to claim superiority, or more rude than for another to dispute the claim. Such differences of station should, if they exist, be taken for granted.

Relations which were established by force may, after a time, be made so beautiful that their origin is forgotten. There must be no display of unnecessary force. The battle having been decided, victor and vanquished change parts. It pleases the conqueror to sign himself, "Your obedient servant," and to inquire whether certain terms would be agreeable. Of course they would be agreeable. So says the disarmed man looking upward to his late foe, now become his protector.

And the conqueror with grave good will takes up the burden which Providence has imposed upon him. Is not the motto of the true knight, *Ich dien?* Such service as he can render shall be given ungrudgingly.

Now, this is not hypocrisy. It may be Christianity and Chivalry and all sorts of fine things. It is making the best of an accepted situation. When relations which were established by force have been sanctioned by custom, and embodied in law, and sanctified by religion, they form a soil in which many pleasant things may grow. In the vicinity of Vesuvius they will tell you that the best soils are of volcanic origin.

Hodge and Sir Lionel meet in the garden which one owns, and in which the other digs with the sweat of his brow. There is kindly interest on the one hand, and decent respect on the other. But all this sense of ordered righteousness is dependent on one condition. Neither must eat of the fruit of the tree of knowledge that grows in the midst of the garden. A little knowledge is dangerous, a good deal of knowledge may be even more dangerous, to the relations which custom has established.

What right has Sir Lionel to lay down the law for Hodge? Why should not Hodge have a right to have his point of view considered? When Hodge begins seriously to ponder this question his manners suffer. And when Sir Lionel begins to assert his superiority, instead of taking it for granted, his behavior lacks its easy charm. It is very hard to explain such things in a gentlemanly way.

Now, the exasperation in the tone of political discussion in Great Britain, as elsewhere in the world, is largely explained by the fact that all sorts of superiorities have been challenged at the same time. Everywhere the issue is sharply made. "Who shall rule?"

Shall Ireland any longer submit to be ruled by the English? The Irish Nationalists swear by all the saints that, rather than submit, they will overthrow the present Government and return to their former methods of agitation.

If the Home Rule Bill be enacted into law, will Ulster submit to be ruled by a Catholic majority? The men of Ulster call upon the spirits of their heroic sires, who triumphed at the Boyne, to bear witness that they will never yield.

Will the masses of the people submit any longer to the existing inequalities in political representation? No! They demand immediate recognition of the principle, "One man, one vote." The many will not allow the few to make laws for them.

Will the women of England kindly wait a little till their demands can be considered in a dignified way? No! They will not take their place in the waiting-line. Others get what they want by pushing; so will they.

Will the Labor party be a little less noisy and insistent in its demands? All will come in time, but one Reform must say to another, "After you." Hoarse voices cry, "We care nothing for etiquette, we must have what we demand, and have it at once. We cannot stand still. If we are pushing, we are also pushed from behind. If you do not give us what we ask for, the Socialists and the Syndicalists will be upon you." There is always the threat of a General Strike. Laborers have hitherto been starved into submission. But two can play at that game.

IV

This is not the England of Sir Roger de Coverley with its cheerful contentment with the actual, and its deference for all sorts of dignitaries. It is not, in its present temper, a model of propriety. But, in my judgment, it is all the more interesting, and full of hope. To say that England is in the midst of a revolution is not to say that some dreadful disaster is impending. It only means that this is a time when events move very rapidly, and when precedents count for little. But it is a time when common sense and courage and energy count for a great deal; and there is no evidence that these qualities are lacking. I suspect that the alarmists are not so alarmed as their language would lead us to suppose. They know their countrymen, and that they have the good sense to avoid most of the collisions that they declare to be inevitable.

I take comfort in the philosophy which I glean from the top of a London motor-bus. From my point of vantage I look down upon pedestrian humanity as a Superman might look down upon it. It seems to consist of a vast multitude of ignorant folk who are predestined to immediate annihilation. As the ungainly machine on which I am seated rushes down the street, it seems admirably adapted for its mission of destruction. The barricade in front of me, devoted to the praise of BOVRIL, is just high enough to prevent my seeing what actually happens, but it gives a blood-curdling view of catastrophes that are imminent. I have an impression of a procession of innocent victims rushing heedlessly upon destruction. Three yards in front of the onrushing wheels is an old gentleman crossing the street. He suddenly stops. There is, humanly speaking, no hope for him. Two nursemaids appear in the field of danger. A butcher's boy on a bicycle steers directly for the bus. He may be given up for lost. I am not able to see what becomes of them, but I am prepared for the worst. Still the expected crunch does not come, and the bus goes on.

Between Notting Hill Gate and Charing Cross I have seen eighteen persons disappear in this mysterious fashion. I could swear that when I last saw them it seemed too late for them to escape their doom.

But on sober reflection I come to the conclusion that I should have taken a more hopeful view if I had not been so high up; if, for example, I had been sitting with the driver where I could have seen what happened at the last moment.

There was much comfort in the old couplet:—

> " Betwixt the saddle and the ground,
> He mercy sought and mercy found."

And betwixt the pedestrian and the motor-bus, there are many chances of safety that I could not foresee. The old gentleman was perhaps more spry than he looked. The nursemaids and the

butcher's boy must assuredly have perished unless they happened to have their wits about them.
But in all probability they did have their wits
about them, and so did the driver of the motor-
bus.

THE TORYISM OF TRAVELERS

✦✦✦✦

I

WHEN we think of a thorough-going conservative we are likely to picture him as a
stay-at-home person, a barnacle fastened to one
spot. We take for granted that aversion to loco-
motion and aversion to change are the same thing.
But in thinking thus we leave out of account the
inherent instability of human nature. Everybody
likes a little change now and then. If a person
cannot get it in one way, he gets it in another.
The stay-at-home gratifies his wandering fancy by
making little alterations in his too-familiar sur-
roundings. Even the Vicar of Wakefield in the
days of his placid prosperity would occasionally
migrate from the blue bed to the brown. A life
that had such vicissitudes could not be called un-
eventful.

When you read the weekly newspaper published in the quietest hill-town in Vermont, you
become aware that a great deal is going on. Dea-

con Pratt shingled his barn last week. Miss Maria Jones had new shutters put on her house, and it is a great improvement. These revolutions in Goshenville are matters of keen interest to those concerned. They furnish inexhaustible material for conversation.

The true enemy to innovation is the traveler who sets out to see historic lands. His natural love of change is satiated by rapid change of locality. But his natural conservatism asserts itself in his insistence that the places which he visits shall be true to their own reputations. Having journeyed, at considerable expense, to a celebrated spot, he wants to see the thing it was celebrated for, and he will accept no substitute. From his point of view the present inhabitants are merely caretakers who should not be allowed to disturb the remains intrusted to their custody. Everything must be kept as it used to be.

The moment any one packs his trunk and puts money in his purse to visit lands old in story he becomes a hopeless reactionary. He is sallying forth to see things not as they are, but as they were " once upon a time." He is attracted to certain localities by something which happened long ago. A great many things may have happened since, but these must be put out of the way. One period of time must be preserved to satisfy his romantic imagination. He loves the good old ways, and he has a curiosity to see the bad old ways that may still be preserved. It is only the modern that offends him.

The American who, in his own country, is in feverish haste to improve conditions, when he sets foot in Europe becomes the fanatical foe to progress. The Old World, in his judgment, ought to look old. He longs to hear the clatter of wooden shoes. If he had his way he would have laws enacted forbidding peasant folk to change their ancient costumes. He would preserve every relic of feudalism. He bitterly laments the division of great estates. A nobleman's park with its beautiful idle acres, its deer, its pheasants, and its scurrying rabbits, is so much more pleasant to look at than a succession of market-gardens. Poachers, game-keepers, and squires are alike interesting, if only they would dress so that he could know them apart. He is enchanted with thatched cottages which look damp and picturesque. He detests the model dwellings which are built with a too-obvious regard for sanitation. He seeks narrow and ill-smelling streets where the houses nod at each other, as if in the last stages of senility, muttering mysterious reminiscences of old tragedies. He frequents scenes of ancient murders, and places where bandits once did congregate. He leaves the railway carriage, to cross a heath where romantic highwaymen used to ask the traveler to stand and deliver. He is indignant to find electric lights and policemen. A heath ought to be lonely, and fens ought to be preserved from drainage.

He seeks dungeons and instruments of torture. The dungeons must be underground, and only a single ray of light must penetrate. He is much troubled to find that the dungeon in the Castle of Chillon is much more cheerful than he had supposed it was. The Bridge of Sighs in Venice disappoints him in the same way. Indeed, there are few places mentioned by Lord Byron that are as gloomy as they are in the poetical description.

The traveler is very insistent in his plea for the preservation of battlefields. Now, Europe is very rich in battlefields, many of the most fertile sections having been fought over many times. But the ravages of agriculture are everywhere seen. There is no such leveler as the ploughman. Often when one has come to refresh his mind with the events of one terrible day, he finds that there is nothing whatever to remind him of what happened. For centuries there has been ploughing and harvesting. Nature takes so kindly to these peaceful pursuits that one is tempted to think of the battle as merely an episode.

Commerce is almost as destructive. Cities that have been noted for their sieges often turn out to be surprisingly prosperous. The old walls are torn down to give way to parks and boulevards. Massacres which in their day were noted leave no trace behind. One can get more of an idea of the Massacre of St. Bartholomew's Eve by reading a book by one's fireside than by going to Paris. For all one can see there, there might have been no such accident.

Moral considerations have little place in the traveler's mind. The progressive ameliorations that have taken place tend to obscure our sense of the old conflicts. A reform once accomplished becomes a part of our ordinary consciousness. We take it for granted, and find it hard to understand what the reformer was so excited about.

As a consequence, the chief object of an historical pilgrimage is to discover some place where the old conditions have not been improved away. The religious pilgrim does not expect to find the old prophets, but he has a pious hope of finding the abuses which the prophets denounced.

I have in mind a clergyman who, in his own home, is progressive to a fault. He is impatient of any delay. He is all the time seeking out the very latest inventions in social and economic reforms. But several years ago he made a journey to the Holy Land, and when he came back he delivered a lecture on his experiences. A more reactionary attitude could not be imagined. Not a word did he say about the progress of education or civil-service reform in Palestine. There was not a sympathetic reference to sanitation or good roads. The rights of women were not mentioned. Representative government seemed to be an abomination to him. All his enthusiasm was for the other side. He was for Oriental conservatism in all its forms. He was for preserving every survival of ancient custom. He told of the delight with which he watched the laborious efforts of the peasants ploughing with a forked stick. He believed that there had not been a single improvement in agriculture since the days of Abraham.

The economic condition of the people had not changed for the better since patriarchal times, and one could still have a good idea of a famine such as sent the brothers of Joseph down into Egypt. Turkish misgovernment furnished him with a much clearer idea of the publicans, and the hatred they aroused in the minds of the people, than he had ever hoped to obtain. In fact, one could hardly appreciate the term "publicans and sinners" without seeing the Oriental tax-gatherers. He was very fortunate in being able to visit several villages which had been impoverished by their exactions. The rate of wages throws much light on the Sunday-School lessons. A penny a day does not seem such an insufficient minimum wage to a traveler, as it does to a stay-at-home person. On going down from Jerusalem to Jericho he fell among thieves, or at least among a group of thievish-looking Bedouins who gave him a new appreciation of the parable of the Samaritan. It was a wonderful experience. And he found that the animosity between the Jews and the Samaritans had not abated. To be sure, there are very few Samaritans left, and those few are thoroughly despised.

The good-roads movement has not yet invaded Palestine, and we can still experience all the discomforts of the earlier times. Many a time when he took his life in his hands and wandered across the Judæan hills, my friend repeated to himself the text, "In the days of Shamgar the son of Anath, in the days of Jael, the highways were unoccupied, and the people walked through by-ways."

To most people Shamgar is a mere name. But after you have walked for hours over those rocky by-ways, never knowing at what moment you may be attacked by a treacherous robber, you know how Shamgar felt. He becomes a real person. You are carried back into the days when "there was no king in Israel, but every man did that which was right in his own eyes."

The railway between Joppa and Jerusalem is to be regretted, but fortunately it is a small affair. There are rumors of commercial enterprises which, if successful, would change the appearance of many of the towns. Fortunately they are not likely to be successful, at least in our day. The brooding spirit of the East can be trusted to defend itself against the innovating West. For the present, at least, Palestine is a fascinating country to travel in.

A traveler in Ceylon and India writes to a religious paper of his journey. He says, " Colombo has little to interest the tourist, yet it is a fine city." One who reads between the lines understands that the fact that it is a fine city is the cause of its uninterestingness. His impression of Madura was more satisfactory. There one can see the Juggernaut car drawn through the streets by a thousand men, though it is reluctantly admitted that the self-immolation of fanatics under the wheels is no longer allowed. "The Shiva temple at Madura is the more interesting as its towers are ornamented with six thousand idols."

The writer who rejoiced at the sight of six thousand idols in Madura, would have been shocked at the exhibition of a single crucifix in his meeting-house at home.

I confess that I have not been able to overcome the Tory prejudice in favor of vested interests in historical places. If one has traveled to

see " the old paths which wicked men have trod-
den," it is a disappointment to find that they are
not there. I had such an experience in Capri.
We had wandered through the vineyards and up
the steep, rocky way to the Villa of Tiberius. On
the top of the cliff are the ruins of the pleasure-
house which the Emperor in his wicked old age
built for himself. Was there ever a greater contrast between an earthly paradise and abounding
sinfulness? Here, indeed, was "spiritual wickedness in high places." The marvelously blue sea
and all the glories of the Bay of Naples ought to
have made Tiberius a better man; but apparently
they didn't. We were prepared for the thrilling
moment when we were led to the edge of the cliff,
and told to look down. Here was the very place
where Tiberius amused himself by throwing his
slaves into the sea to feed the fishes. Cruel old
monster! But it was a long time ago. Time had
marvelously softened the atrocity of the act, and
heightened its picturesque character. If Tiberius
must exhibit his colossal inhumanity, could he
have anywhere in all the world chosen a better
spot? Just think of his coming to this island
and, on this high cliff above the azure sea, build-

ing this palace! And then to think of him on a night when the moon was full, and the nightingales were singing, coming out and hurling a shuddering slave into the abyss!

When we returned to the hotel, our friend the Professor, who had made a study of the subject, informed us that it was all a mistake. The stories of the wicked doings of Tiberius in Capri were malicious slanders. The Emperor was an elderly invalid living in dignified retirement. As for the slaves, we might set our minds at rest in regard to them. If any of them fell over the cliff it was pure accident. We must give up the idea that the invalid Emperor pushed them off.

All this was reassuring to my better nature, and yet I cherished a grudge against the Professor. For it was a stiff climb to the Villa of Tiberius, and I wanted something to show for it. It was difficult to adjust one's mind to the fact that nothing had happened there which might not have happened in any well-conducted country house.

I like to contrast this with our experience in Algiers. We knew beforehand what Algiers was like in the days of its prime. It had been the nest of as desperate pirates as ever infested the seas. For generations innocent Christians had been carried hither to pine in doleful captivity. But the French, we understood, had built a miniature Paris in the vicinity and were practicing liberty, fraternity, and equality on the spot dedicated to gloomily romantic memories. We feared the effect of this civilization. We had our misgivings. Perhaps Algiers might be no longer worth visiting.

Luckily our steamer was delayed till sunset. We were carefully shepherded, so that we hardly noticed the French city. We were hurried through the darkness into old Algiers. Everything was full of sinister suggestion. The streets were as narrow and perilous as any which Haroun Al Raschid explored on his more perilous nights. Here one could believe the worst of his fellow men. Suspicion and revenge were in the air. We were not taking a stroll, we were escaping from something. Mysterious muffled figures glided by and disappeared through slits in the walls. There were dark corners so suggestive of homicide that one could hardly think that any one with an Oriental disposition could resist the temptation. In crypt-like recesses we could see assassins sharpening their daggers or, perhaps, executioners putting the finishing touches on their scimitars. There were cavernous rooms where conspirators were crouched round a tiny charcoal fire. Groups of truculent young Arabs followed us shouting objurgations, and accepting small coins as ransom. We had glimpses of a mosque, the outside of a prison, and the inside of what once was a harem. On returning to the steamer one gentleman fell overboard and, swimming to the shore, was rescued by a swarthy ruffian who robbed him of his watch and disappeared in the darkness. When the victim of Algerian piracy stood on the deck, dripping and indignant, and told his tale of woe, we were delighted. Algiers would always be something to remember. It was one of the places that had not been spoiled.

I am afraid that the sunlight might have brought disillusion. Some of the stealthy figures which gave rise to such thrilling suspicions may have turned out to be excellent fathers and husbands returning from business. As it is, thanks to the darkness, Algiers remains a city of vague atrocities. It does not belong to the commonplace world; it is of such stuff as dreams, including nightmares, are made of.

It is not without some compunction of conscience that I recall two historical pilgrimages, one to Assisi, the other to Geneva. Assisi I found altogether rewarding, while in Geneva I was disappointed. In each case my object was purely selfish, and had nothing in common with the welfare of the present inhabitants. I wanted to see the city of St. Francis and the city of John Calvin.

In Assisi one may read again the Franciscan legends in their proper settings. I should like to think that my pleasure in Assisi arose from the fact that I saw some one there who reminded me of St. Francis. But I was not so fortunate. If one is anxious to come in contact with the spirit of St. Francis, freed from its mediæval limitations, a visit to Hull House, Chicago, would be more rewarding.

But it was not the spirit of St. Francis, but his limitations, that we were after. Assisi has preserved them all. We see the gray old town on the hillside, the narrow streets, the old walls. We are beset by swarms of beggars. They are not like the half-starved creatures one may see in the slums of northern cities. They are very likable. They are natural worshipers of my Lady Poverty. They have not been spoiled by commonplace industrialism or scientific philanthropy. One is taken back into the days when there was a natural affinity between saints and beggars. The saints would joyously give away all that they had, and the beggars would as joyously accept it. After the beggars had used up all the saints had given them, the saints would go out and beg for more. The community, you say, would be none the better. Perhaps not. But the moment you begin to talk about the community you introduce ideas that are modern and disturbing. One thing is certain, and that is that if Assisi were more thrifty, it would be less illuminating historically.

St. Francis might come back to Assisi and take up his work as he left it. But I sought in vain for John Calvin in Geneva. The city was too prosperous and gay. The cheerful houses, the streets with their cosmopolitan crowds, the parks, the schools, the university, the little boats skimming over the lake, all bore witness to the well-being of to-day. But what of yesterday? The citizens were celebrating the anniversary of Jean Jacques Rousseau. I realized that it was not yesterday but the day before yesterday that I was seeking. Where was the stern little city which Calvin taught and ruled? The place that knew him knows him no more.

Disappointed in my search for Calvin, I sought compensation in Servetus. I found the stone placed by modern Calvinists to mark the spot where the Spanish heretic was burned. On it they had carved an inscription expressing their regret for the act of intolerance on the part of the reformer, and attributing the blame to the age in which he lived. But even this did not satisfy modern Geneva. The inscription had been chipped away in order to give place I was told, to something more historically accurate.

But whether Calvin was to blame, or the sixteenth century, did not seem to matter. The spot was so beautiful that it seemed impossible that anything tragical could ever have happened here. A youth and maiden were sitting by the stone, engaged in a most absorbing conversation. Of one thing I was certain, that the theological differences between Calvin and Servetus were nothing to them. They had something more important to think about — at least for them.

II

After a time one comes to have a certain modesty of expectation. Time and Space are different elements, and each has its own laws. At the price of a steamship ticket one may be transported to another country, but safe passage to another age is not guaranteed. It is enough if some slight suggestion is given to the imagination. A walk through a pleasant neighborhood is all the pleasanter if one knows that something memorable has happened there. If one is wise he will not attempt to realize it to the exclusion of the present scene. It is enough to have a slight flavor of historicity.

It was this pleasure which I enjoyed in a ramble with a friend through the New Forest. The day was fine, and it would have been a joy to be under the greenwood trees if no one had been before us. But the New Forest had a human interest; for on such a day as this, William Rufus rode into it to hunt the red deer, and was found with an arrow through his body. And to this day no man knows who killed William Rufus, or why. Though, of course, some people have their suspicions.

Many other things may have happened in the New Forest in the centuries that have passed, but they have never been brought vividly to my attention. So far as I was concerned there were no confusing incidents. The Muse of History told one tragic tale and then was silent.

On the other side of the Forest was the Rufus stone marking the spot where the Red King's body was found. At Brockenhurst we inquired the way, which we carefully avoided. The road itself was an innovation, and was infested with motor-cars, machines unknown to the Normans. The Red King had plunged into the Forest and quickly lost himself; so would we. There were great oaks and wide-spreading beeches and green glades such as one finds only in England. It was pleasant to feel that it all belonged to the Crown. I could not imagine a county council allowing this great stretch of country to remain in its unspoiled beauty through these centuries.

We took our frugal lunch under a tree that

had looked down on many generations. Then we wandered on through a green wilderness. We saw no one but some women gathering fagots. I was glad to see that they were exercising their ancestral rights in the royal domain. They looked contented, though I should have preferred to have their dress more antique.

All day we followed William Rufus through the Forest. I began to feel that I had a real acquaintance with him, having passed through much the same experience. The forest glades have been little changed since the day when he hunted the red deer. Nature is the true conservative, and repeats herself incessantly.

Toward evening my friend pointed out the hill at the foot of which was the Rufus stone. It was still some two miles away. Should we push on to it?

What should we see when we got there? The stone was not much. There was a railing round it as a protection against relic-hunters. And there was an inscription which, of course, was comparatively modern. That settled it. We would not go to the stone with its modern inscription. The ancient trees brought us much nearer to

William Rufus. Besides, there was just time, if we walked briskly, to catch the train at Brocken-hurst.

III

A week which stands out in my memory as one of perfect communion with the past was spent with another English friend in Llanthony Abbey, in the Vale of Ewyas, in the Black Mountains of Wales. We had gone prepared for camping with a tent of ethereal lightness, which was to protect us from the weather.

For the first night we were to tarry amid the ruins of the twelfth-century abbey, some parts of which had been roofed over and used as an inn. When we arrived, the rain was falling in torrents. Soon after supper we took our candles and climbed the winding stone stairs to our rooms in the tower. The stones were uneven and worn by generations of pious feet. Outside we could see the ruined nave of the church, with all the surrounding buildings. We were in another age.

Had the sun shined next morning we should have gone on our gypsy journey, and Llanthony

Abbey would have been only an incident. But for five days and five nights the rain descended. We could make valiant sallies, but were driven back for shelter. Shut in by " the tumultuous privacy of storm," one felt a sense of ownership. Only one book could be obtained, the " Life and Letters " of Walter Savage Landor. I had always wanted to know more of Landor and here was the opportunity.

A little over a hundred years ago he came to the vale of Ewyas and bought this estate, and hither he brought his young bride. They occupied our rooms, it appeared. In 1809, Landor writes to Southey, " I am about to do what no man hath ever done in England, plant a wood of cedars of Lebanon. These trees will look magnificent on the mountains of Llanthony." He planted a million of them, so he said. How eloquently he growled over those trees! He prophesied that none of them would live.

After reading, I donned my raincoat and started out through the driving storm to see how Landor's trees were getting on. It seemed that it was only yesterday that they were planted. It was worth going out to see what had become of them. They were all gone. I felt that secret satisfaction which all right-minded persons feel on being witnesses to the fulfilment of prophecy.

And then there was the house which Landor started to build when he and his wife were living in our tower. " I hope," he writes, " before the close not of the next but of the succeeding summer, to have one room to sit in with two or three bedrooms." Then he begins to growl about the weather and the carpenters. After a while he writes again of the house: " It's not half finished and has cost me two thousand pounds. I think seriously of filling it with straw and setting fire to it. Never was anything half so ugly."

I inquired about the house and was told that it was not far away on the hillside, and was yet unfinished. I was pleased with this, and meant to go up and see it when the spell of bad weather of which Landor complained had passed by.

Beside Landor there was only one other historic association which one could enjoy without getting drenched — that was St. David. In wading across the barnyard, I encountered "Boots," an intelligent young man though unduly respectful. He informed me that the old building just across from the stable was the cell of St. David.

I was not prepared for this. All I knew was that St. David was the patron saint of Wales and had a cathedral and a number of other churches dedicated to him. Without too grossly admitting my ignorance, I tried to draw out from my mentor some further biographical facts that my imagination might work on during my stay. He thought that St. David was some relation to King Arthur, but just what the relation was, and whether he was only a relative by marriage, he didn't know. It wasn't very much information, but I was profoundly grateful to him.

I have since read a long article on St. David in the "Cambrian Plutarch." The author goes into the question of the family relations between King Arthur and St. David with great thoroughness, but what conclusion he comes to is not quite evident. He thinks that the people are wrong who say that St. David was a nephew, because he was fifty years older than Arthur. That would make him more likely his uncle. But as he admits that King Arthur may possibly be another name for the constellation Ursa Major, it is difficult to fix the dates exactly. At any rate, the "Cambrian Plutarch" is sure that King Arthur was a Welshman and a credit to the country — and so was St. David. The author was as accurate in regard to the dates as the nature of his subject would allow. He adds apologetically, "It will appear that the life of St. David is rather misplaced with respect to chronological order. But as he was contemporary with all those whose lives have already been given, the anachronism, if such it may be called, can be of no great importance."

That is just the way I feel about it. After living for a whole week in such close contact with the residence of St. David, I feel a real interest in him. Just who he was and when he lived, if at all, is a matter of no great importance.

Yet there are limits to the historical imagination. It must have something to work on, even though that something may be very vague. We must draw the line somewhere in our pursuit of antiquity. A relic may be too old to be effective. Instead of gently stimulating the imagination it may paralyze it. What we desire is not merely the ancient but the familiar. The relic must bring with it the sense of auld lang-syne. The Tory squire likes to preserve what has been a long time in his family. The traveler has the same feeling for the possessions of the family of humanity.

The family-feeling does not go back of a certain point. I draw the line at the legendary period when the heroes have names, and more or less coherent stories are told of their exploits. People who had a local habitation, but not a name, seem to belong to Geology only. For all their flint arrow-heads, or bronze instruments, I cannot think of them as fellow men.

It was with this feeling that I visited one of the most ancient places of worship in Ireland, the tumulus at Newgrange. It was on a day filled with historic sight-seeing. We started from Drogheda, the great stronghold of the Pale in the Middle Ages, and the scene of Cromwell's terrible vengeance in 1649. Three miles up the river is the site of the Battle of the Boyne. It was one of the great indecisive battles of the world, it being necessary to fight it over again every year. The Boyne had overflowed its banks, and in the fields forlorn hay-cocks stood like so many little islands. We stopped at the battle monument and read its Whiggish inscription, which was scorned by our honest driver. We could form some idea of how the field appeared on the eventful day when King William and King James confronted each other across the narrow stream. Then the scene changed and we found ourselves in Mellefont Abbey, the first Cistercian monastery in Ireland, founded by St. Malachy, the friend of St. Bernard of Clairvaux. King William and King James were at once relegated to their proper places among the moderns, while we went back to the ages of faith.

Four miles farther we came to Monasterboice, where stood two great Celtic crosses. There are two ruined churches and a round tower. Here was an early religious establishment which existed before the times of St. Columba.

This would be enough for one day's reminiscence, but my heart leaped up at the sight of a long green ridge. "There is the hill of Tara!"

Having traversed the period from King William to the dwellers in the Halls of Tara, what more natural than to take a further plunge into the past?

We drive into an open field and alight near a rock-strewn hill. Candles are given us and we grope our way through narrow passages till we come to the centre of the hill. Here is a chamber some twenty feet in height. On the great stones which support the roof are mystic emblems. On the floor is a large stone hollowed out in the shape of a bowl. It suggests human sacrifices. My guide did not encourage this suggestion. There was, he thought, no historical evidence for it. But it seemed to me that if these people ever practised such sacrifices this was the place for them. A gloomier chamber for weird rites could not be imagined.

Who were the worshipers? Druids or pre-Druids? The archæologists tell us that they belonged to the Early Bronze period. Now Early Bronze is a good enough term for articles in a museum, but it does not suggest a human being. We cannot get on terms of spiritual intimacy with the Early Bronze people. We may know what they did, but there is no intimation of " the moving why they did it." What spurred them on to their feats of prodigious industry? Was it fear or love? First they built their chapel of great stones and then piled a huge hill on top of it. Were they still under the influence of the glacial period and attempting to imitate the wild doings of Nature? The passage of the ages does not make these men seem venerable, because their deeds are no longer intelligible. Mellefont Abbey is in ruins, but we can easily restore it in imagination. We can picture the great buildings as they were before the iconoclasts destroyed them. The prehistoric place of worship in the middle of the hill is practically unchanged. But the clue to its meaning is lost.

I could not make the ancient builders and worshipers seem real. It was a relief to come up into the sunshine where people of our own kind had walked, the Kings of Tara and their harpers, and St. Patrick and St. Malachy and Oliver Cromwell and William III. After the unintelligible symbols on the rocks, how familiar and homelike seemed the sculptures on the Celtic crosses. They were mostly about people, and people whom we had known from earliest childhood. There were Adam and Eve, and Cain slaying Abel, and the Magi. They were members of our family.

But between us and the builders of the underground chapel there was a great gulf. There was no means of spiritual communication across the abyss. A scrap of writing, a bit of poetry, a name handed down by tradition, would have been worth all the relics discovered by archæologists.

There is justification for the traveler's preference for the things he has read about, for these are the things which resist the changes of time. Only he must remember that they are better preserved in the book than in the places where they happened. The impression which any generation makes on the surface of the earth is very slight. It cannot give the true story of the brief occupancy. That requires some more direct interpretation.

The magic carpet which carries us into any age not our own is woven by the poets and historians. Without their aid we may travel through Space, but not through Time.

THE OBVIOUSNESS OF DICKENS

❖❖❖❖

IN the college world it is a point of honor for the successive classes to treat each other with contumely. The feud between freshman and sophomore goes on automatically. Only when one has become a senior may he, without losing caste, recognize a freshman as a youth of promise, and admit that a sophomore is not half bad. Such disinterested criticism is tolerated because it is evidently the result of the mellowing influence of time.

The same tendency is seen in literary and artistic judgments. It is never good taste to admit the good taste of the generation that immediately precedes us. Its innocent admirations are flouted and its standards are condemned as provincial. For we are always emerging from the dark ages and contrasting their obscurity with our marvelous light. The sixteenth century scorned the fifteenth century for its manifold superstitions. Thomas Fuller tells us that his enlightened contemporaries in the seventeenth century treated the enthusiasms of the sixteenth century with scant respect. The price of martyrs' ashes rises and falls in Smithfield market. At a later period Pope writes, —

> " We think our fathers fools, so wise we grow:
> Our wiser sons, perhaps, will think us so."

He need not have put in the "perhaps."

The nineteenth century had its fling at the artificiality of the eighteenth century, and treated it with contempt as the age of doctrinaires. And now that the twentieth century is coming to the age of discretion, we hear a new term of reproach, Mid-Victorian. It expresses the sum of all villainies in taste. For some fifty years in the nineteenth century the English-speaking race, as it now appears, was under the sway of Mrs. Grundy. It was living in a state of most reprehensible respectability, and Art was tied to the apron-strings of Morality. Everybody admired what ought not to be admired. We are only now beginning to pass judgment on the manifold mediocrity of this era.

All this must, for the time, count against Dickens; for of all the Victorians he was the midmost.

He flourished in that most absurd period of time —the time just before most of us were born. And how he did flourish! Grave lord chancellors confessed to weeping over Little Nell. A Mid-Victorian bishop relates that after administering consolation to a man in his last illness he heard him saying, "At any rate, a new 'Pickwick Paper' will be out in ten days."

Everywhere there was a wave of hysterical appreciation. Describing his reading in Glasgow, Dickens writes: "Such pouring of hundreds into a place already full to the throat, such indescribable confusion, such rending and tearing of dresses, and yet such a scene of good humor, I never saw the slightest approach to. . . . Fifty frantic men got up in all parts of the hall and addressed me all at once. Other frantic men made speeches to the wall. The whole B family were borne on the top of a wave and landed with their faces against the front of the platform. I read with the platform crammed with people. I got them to lie down upon it, and it was like some impossible tableau, or gigantic picnic, — one pretty girl lying on her side all night, holding on to the legs of my table."

In New York eager seekers after fiction would "lie down on the pavement the whole of the night before the tickets were sold, generally taking up their position about ten." There would be free fights, and the police would be called to quell the riot.

Such astonishing actions on the part of people who were unfortunate enough to live in the middle of the nineteenth century put us on our guard. It could not have been a serious interest in English literature that evoked the mob spirit. Dickens must have been writing the kind of books which these people liked to hear read. We remember with some misgivings that in the days of our youth we wept over Little Nell, just as the lord chancellor did. The question which disturbs us is, Ought we to have done so?

Let us by a soft answer turn away the wrath of the critic. Doubtless we ought not to have done so. Our excuse is that, at the time, we could not help it. We may make the further plea, common to all soft-hearted sinners, that if we had n't wept, other people would, so that no great harm was done, after all.

But letting bygones be bygones, and not seeking to justify the enthusiasms of the nineteenth century, one may return to Dickens as to the home of one's childhood. How do the old scenes affect us? Does the charm remain? When thus we return to Dickens, we are compelled to confess the justice of the latter-day criticism. In all his writings he deals with characters and situations which are wholly obvious; at least they are obvious after he deals with them. Not only is he without the art which conceals art, but, unlike some novelists of more recent fame, he is without the art that conceals the lack of art. He produces an impression by the crude method of "rubbing it in." There are no subtleties to pique our curiosity, no problems left us for discussion, no room for difference of opinion. There is no more opportunity for speculation than in a one-price clothing store where every article is marked in plain figures. To have heartily disliked Mr. Pecksniff and to have loved the Cheeryble Brothers indicates no sagacity on our part. The author has distinctly and repeatedly told us that the one is an odious hypocrite and that the others are benevolent to an unusual degree. Our appreciation of Sam Weller does not prove that we have any sense of humor save that which is common to man. For Mr. Weller's humor is a blessing that is not in disguise. It is a pump which needs no priming. There is no denying that the humor, the pathos, and the sentiment of Dickens are obvious.

All this, according to certain critics, goes to prove that Dickens lacks distinction, and that the writing of his novels was a commonplace achievement. This judgment seems to me to arise from a confusion of thought. The *perception* of the obvious is a commonplace achievement; the *creation* of the obvious, and making it interesting, is the work of genius. There is no intellectual distinction in the enjoyment of "The Pickwick Papers"; to write "The Pickwick Papers" would be another matter.

It is only in the last quarter of a century that English literature has been accepted not as a recreation, but as a subject of serious study. Now, the first necessity for a study is that it should be "hard." Some of the best brains in the educational world have been enlisted in the work of giving a disciplinary value to what was originally an innocent pleasure. It is evident that one cannot give marks for the number of smiles or tears evoked by a tale of true love. The novel or the play that is to hold its own in the curriculum in competition with trigonometry must have some knotty problem which causes the harassed reader to knit his brows in anxious thought.

In answer to this demand, the literary craftsman has arisen who takes his art with a seriousness which makes the "painful preacher" of the Puritan time seem a mere pleasure-seeker. Equipped with instruments of precision drawn from the psychological laboratory, he is prepared to satisfy our craving for the difficult. By the method of suggestion he tries to make us believe that we have never seen his characters before, and sometimes he succeeds. He deals in descriptions which leave us with the impression of an indescribable something which we should recognize if we were as clever as he is. As we are not nearly so clever, we are left with a chastened sense of our inferiority, which is doubtless good for us. And all this groping for the un-obvious is connected with an equally insistent demand for realism. The novel must not only be as real as life, but it must be more so. For life, as it appears in our ordinary consciousness, is full of illusions. When these are stripped off and the residuum is compressed into a book, we have that which is at once intensely real and painfully unfamiliar.

Now, there is a certain justification for this. A psychologist may show us aspects of character which we could not see by ourselves, as the X-rays will reveal what is not visible to the naked eye. But if the insides of things are real, so also are the outsides. Surfaces and forms are not without their importance.

It may be said in extenuation of Dickens that the blemish of obviousness is one which he shared with the world he lived in. It would be too much to say that all realities are obvious. There is a great deal that we do not see at the first glance; but there is a great deal that we do see. To reproduce the freshness and wonder of the first view of the obvious world is one of the greatest achievements of the imagination.

The reason why the literary artist shuns the obvious is that there is too much of it. It is too big for the limited resources of his art. In the actual world, realities come in big chunks. Nature continually repeats herself. She hammers her facts into our heads with a persistency which is often more than a match for our stupidity. If we do not recognize a fact to-day, it will hit us in the same place to-morrow.

We are so used to this educational method of reiteration that we make it a test of reality. An impression made upon us must be repeated before it has validity to our reason. If a thing really happened, we argue that it will happen again under the same conditions. That is what we mean by saying that we are under the reign of law. There is a great family resemblance between happenings.

We make acquaintance with people by the same method. The recognition of identity depends upon the ability which most persons have of appearing to be remarkably like themselves. The reason why we think that the person whom we met to-day is the same person we met yesterday is that he *seems* the same. There are obvious resemblances that strike us at once. He looks the same, he acts the same, he has the same mannerisms, the same kind of voice, and he answers to the same name. If Proteus, with the best intention in the world, but with an unlimited variety of self-manifestations, were to call every day, we should greet him always as a stranger. We should never feel at home with so versatile a person. A character must have a certain degree of monotony about it before we can trust it. Unexpectedness is an agreeable element in wit, but not in friendship. Our friend must be one who can say with honest Joe Gargery, "It were understood, and it are understood, and it ever will be similar, according."

But in the use of this effective method of re-iteration there is a difference between nature and a book. Nature does not care whether she bores us or not: she has us by the buttonhole, and we cannot get away. Not so with a book. When we are bored, we lay it down, and that brings the interview to an end. It is from the fear of our impatience that most writers abstain from the natural method of producing an impression.

And they are quite right. It is only now and then that an audience will grant an extension of time to a speaker in order that he may make his point more clear. They would rather miss the point. And it is still more rare for the reader to grant a similar extension in order that the author may tell again what he has told before. It is much easier to shut up a book than to shut up a speaker.

The criticism of Dickens that his characters repeat themselves quite misses the mark. As well object to an actor that he frequently responds to an encore. If indicted for the offense, he could at least insist that the audience be indicted with him as accessory before the fact.

Dickens tells us that when he read at Harrogate, "There was a remarkably good fellow of thirty or so who found something so very ludicrous in Toots that he could not compose himself at all, but laughed until he sat wiping his eyes with his handkerchief, and whenever he felt Toots coming again he began to laugh and wipe his eyes afresh."

"Whenever he felt Toots coming again" — there you have the whole philosophy of the matter. The young fellow found Toots amusing when he first laid eyes on him. He wanted to see him again, and it must always be the same Toots.

It is useless to cavil at an author because of the means by which he produces his effects. The important thing is that he does produce an effect. That the end justifies the means may be a dangerous doctrine in ethics, but much may be said for it in literature. The situation is like that of a middle-aged gentleman beset by a small boy on a morning just right for snowballing. "Give me leave, mister?" cries the youthful sharp-shooter. The good-natured citizen gives leave by pulling up his coat-collar and quickening his pace. If the small boy can hit him, he is forgiven, if he cannot hit him, he is scorned. The fact is that Dickens with a method as broad and repetitious as that of Nature herself does succeed in hitting our fancy. That is, he succeeds nine times out of ten.

It is the minor characters of Dickens that are remembered. And we remember them for the same reason that we remember certain faces which we have seen in a crowd. There is some salient feature or trick of manner which first attracts and then holds our attention. A person must have some tag by which he is identified, or, so far as we are concerned, he becomes one of the innumerable lost articles. There are persons who are like umbrellas, very useful, but always liable to be forgotten. The memory is an infirm faculty, and must be humored. It often clings to mere trifles. The man with the flamboyant necktie whom you saw on the 8.40 train may also be the author of a volume of exquisite lyrics; but you never saw the lyrics, and you did see the necktie. In the scale of being, the necktie may be the least important parcel of this good man's life, but it is the only thing about him which attracts your attention. When you see it day after day at the same hour you feel that you have a real, though perhaps not a deep, acquaintance with the man behind it. It is thus we habitually perceive the human world. We see things, and infer persons to correspond. One peculiarity attracts us. It is not the whole man, but it is all of him that is for us. In all this we are very Dickensy.

We may read an acute character study and straightway forget the person who was so admirably analyzed; but the lady in the yellow curl-papers is unforgettable. We really see very little of her, but she is real, and she would not be so real without her yellow curl-papers. A yellow-curl-paper-less lady in the Great White Horse

Inn would be as unthinkable to us as a white-plume-less Henry of Navarre at Ivry.

In ecclesiastical art the saints are recognized by their emblems. Why should not the sinners have the same means of identification? Dickens has the courage to furnish us these necessary aids to recollection. Micawber, Mrs. Gummidge, Barkis, Mr. Dick, Uriah Heep, Betsy Trotwood, Dick Swiveller, Mr. Mantalini, Harold Skimpole, Sairey Gamp, always appear with their appropriate insignia. We should remember that it is for our sakes.

According to the canons of literary art, a fact should be stated clearly once and for all. It would be quite proper to mention the fact that Silas Wegg had a wooden leg; but this fact having been made plain, why should it be referred to again? There is a sufficient reason based on sound psychology. If the statement were not repeated, we should forget that Mr. Wegg had a wooden leg, and by and by we should forget Silas Wegg himself. He would fade away among the host of literary gentlemen who are able to read " The Decline and Fall," but who are not able to keep themselves out of the pit of oblivion. But when we repeatedly see Mr. Wegg as Mr. Boffin saw him, "the literary gentleman *with* a wooden leg," we feel that we really have the pleasure of his acquaintance. There is not only perception of him, but what the pedagogical people call apperception. Our idea of Mr. Wegg is inseparably connected with our antecedent ideas of general woodenness.

Again, we are introduced to "a large, hard-breathing, middle-aged man, with a mouth like a fish, dull, staring eyes, and sandy hair standing upright on his head, so that he looked as if he had been choked and had at that moment come to." This is Mr. Pumblechook. He does not emerge slowly like a ship from below the horizon. We see him all at once, eyes, mouth, hair, and character to match. It is a case of falling into acquaintance at first sight. We are now ready to hear what Mr. Pumblechook says and see what he does. We have a reasonable assurance that whatever he says and does it will be just like Mr. Pumblechook.

We enter a respectable house in a shady angle adjoining Portman Square. We go out to dinner in solemn procession. We admire the preternatural solidity of the furniture and the plate. The hostess is a fine woman, " with neck and nostrils like a rocking-horse, hard features and majestic headdress." Her husband, large and pompous, with little light-colored wings "more like hair-brushes than hair" on the sides of his otherwise bald head, begins to discourse on the British Constitution. We now know as much of Mr. Podsnap as we shall know at the end of the book. But it is a real knowledge conveyed by the method that gives dinner-parties their educational value. We forgive Dickens his superfluous discourse on Podsnappery in general. For his remarks are precisely of the kind which we make when the party is over, and we sit by the fire generalizing and allegorizing the people we have met.

That Mr. Thomas Gradgrind was unduly addicted to hard facts might have been delicately insinuated in the course of two hundred pages. We might have felt a mild pleasure in the discovery which we had made, and then have gone our way forgetting what manner of man he was. What is Gradgrind to us or we to Gradgrind? Dickens introduces him to us in all his uncompromising squareness — " square coat, square legs, square shoulders, nay, his very neckcloth is trained to take him by the throat with an unaccommodating grasp." We are made at once to see "the square wall of a forehead which had his eyebrows for its base, while his eyes found commodious cellarage in the two dark caves overshadowed by the wall." Having taken all this in at a glance, there is nothing more to be done in the development of the character of Mr. Gradgrind. He takes his place among the obvious facts of existence. But in so much as we were bound to find him out sometime, shall we quarrel with Dickens because we were enabled to do so in the first chapter?

Nor do the obvious exaggerations of Dickens arising from the exuberance of his fancy interfere with the sense of reality. A truth is not less true because it is in large print. We recognize creatures who are prodigiously like ourselves, and we laugh at the difference in scale. Did not all Lilliput laugh over the discovery of Gulliver? How they rambled over the vast expanse of countenance, recognizing each feature — lips, cheek, nose, chin, brow. "How very odd," they would say to themselves, "and how very like!"

It is to the wholesome obviousness of Dickens

that we owe the atmosphere of good cheer that surrounds his characters. No writer has pictured more scenes of squalid misery, and yet we are not depressed. There is bad weather enough, but we are not "under the weather." There are characters created to be hated. It is a pleasure to hate them. As to the others, whenever their trials and tribulations abate for an instant, they relapse into a state of unabashed contentment.

This is unusual in literature, for most literary men are saddest when they write. The fact is that happiness is much more easy to experience than to describe, as any one may learn in trying to describe a good time he has had. One good time is very much like another good time. Moreover, we are shy, and dislike to express our enthusiasm. We would n't for the world have any one know what simple creatures we are and how little it takes to make us happy. So we talk critically about a great many things we do not care very much about, and complain of the absence of many things which we do not really miss. We feel badly about not being invited to a party which we don't want to go to.

We are like a horse that has been trained to

be a "high-stepper." By prancing over imaginary difficulties and shying at imaginary dangers he gives an impression of mettlesomeness which is foreign to his native disposition.

The story-teller is on the lookout for these eager attitudes. He cannot afford to let his characters be too happy. There is a literary value in misery that he cannot afford to lose.

That "the course of true love never did run smooth" is an assertion of story-tellers rather than of ordinary lovers. The fact is that nothing is so easy as falling in love and staying there. It is a very common experience, so common that it attracts little attention. The course of true love usually runs so smoothly that there is nothing that causes remark. It is not an occasion of gossip. Two good-tempered and healthy persons are obviously made for each other. They know it, and everybody else knows it, and they keep on knowing it, and act, as Joe Gargery would say, "similar, according."

The trouble is that the literary man finds that this does not afford exciting material for a best seller. So he must invent hazards to make the game interesting to the spectators. In a story the course of true love must not run smooth or no one would read it. The old-time romancer brought his young people through all sorts of misadventures. When all the troubles he could think of were over, he left them abruptly at the church door, murmuring feebly to the gentle reader, "they were happy ever after."

The present-day novelist is offended at this ending. "How absurd!" he says. "They are still in the early twenties. The world is all before them, and they have time to fall into all sorts of troubles which the romanticist has not thought of. Middle age is just as dangerous a period as youth, and matrimony has its pitfalls. Let me take up the story and tell you how they did n't live happily ever afterwards, but, on the contrary, had a cat-and-dog life of it."

Now I would pardon the novelist if he were perfectly honest and were to say, "Ladies and gentlemen, I am trying to interest you. I have not the skill to make a story of placid happiness interesting. So I will do the next best thing. I will tell you a story of a different kind. It is the picture of a kind of life that is easier to make readable."

In making such a confession he would be in

good company. Even Shakespeare, with all his dramatic genius, confessed that he could not avoid monotony in his praise of true love. Its ways were ways of pleasantness, but did not afford much incentive to originality.

> " Since all alike my songs and praises be
>   To one, of one, still such, and ever so.
>   Kind is my love to-day, to-morrow kind,
>   Still constant in a wondrous excellence ;
>   Therefore my verse to constancy confined,
>   One thing expressing, leaves out difference.
> ' Fair, kind, and true ' is all my argument,
> ' Fair, kind, and true ' varying to other words ;
>   And in this change is my invention spent.''

But the novelist, when he takes himself too seriously as the man who is to show us "life as it is," is not content to acknowledge his limitations. When he pictures a situation in which there is nothing but a succession of problems and misunderstandings, he asks us to admire his austere faithfulness. Faithful he may be to his Art, as he understands it, but he is not faithful to reality, unless he is able to make us see ordinary people in the act of enjoying themselves.

The most obvious thing in life is that people are seldom as unhappy as their circumstances

would lead us to expect. Nobody is happy all
the time, and if he were, nobody is enough of a
genius to make his undeviating felicity interesting.
But a great many people are happy most of the
time, and almost everybody has been happy at
some time or other. It may have been only a momentary experience, but it was very real, and he
likes to think about it. He is excessively grateful
to any one who recalls the feeling. The point is
that the aggregate of these good times makes a
considerable amount of cheerfulness.

Dickens does not attempt the impossible literary feat of showing us one person who is happy
all the time, but he does what is more obvious,
he makes us see a great many people who have
snatches of good cheer in the midst of their hum-
drum lives. He lets us see another obvious fact,
that happiness is more a matter of temperament
than of circumstance. It is not given as a reward
of merit or as a mark of distinguished consideration. There is one perennial fountain of pleasure.
Any one can have a good time who can *enjoy
himself*. Dickens was not above celebrating the
kind of happiness which comes to the natural
man and the natural boy through what we call the

"creature comforts." He could sympathize with
the unadulterated self-satisfaction of little Jack
Horner when

> " He put in his thumb
> And pulled out a plum,
> And said, ' What a great boy am I ! ' "

The finding of the plum was not a matter of
world-wide importance, but it was a great pleasure for Jack Horner, and he did not care who
knew it.

What joy Mr. Micawber gets out of his own
eloquence! We cannot begrudge him this unearned increment. We sympathize, as, "much
affected, but still intensely enjoying himself, Mr.
Micawber folded up his letter and handed it with
a bow to my aunt as something she might like to
keep."

And R. Wilfer, despite his meagre salary, and
despite Mrs. Wilfer, enjoys himself whenever he
gets a chance. When he goes to Greenwich with
Bella he finds everything as it should be. " Everything was delightful. The Park was delightful;
the punch was delightful, the dishes of fish were
delightful; the wine was delightful." If that was
not happiness, what was it?

Said R. Wilfer: "Supposing a man to go through life, we won't say with a companion, but we will say with a tune. Very good. Supposing the tune allotted to him was the 'Dead March' in 'Saul.' Well. It would be a very suitable tune for particular occasions — none more so — but it would be difficult to keep time with it in the ordinary run of domestic transactions."

It is a matter of common observation that those who have allotted to them the most solemn music do not always keep time with it. In the " ordinary run of domestic transactions " they find many little alleviations. In the aggregate these amount to a considerable blessing. The world may be rough, and many of its ways may be cruel, but for all that it is a joyful sensation to be alive, and the more alive we are, the better we like it. All of which is very obvious, and it is what we want somebody to point out for us again and again.

THE SPOILED CHILDREN OF
CIVILIZATION

◆◆◆◆

TO spoil a child is no easy task, for Nature is all the time working in behalf of the childish virtues and veracities, and is gently correcting the abnormalities of education. Still it can be done. The secret of it is never to let the child alone, and to insist on doing for him all that he would otherwise do for himself — and more.

In that " more " lies the spoiling power. The child must be early made acquainted with the feeling of satiety. There must be too much of everything. If he were left to himself to any extent, this would be an unknown experience. For he is a hungry little creature, with a growing appetite, and naturally is busy ministering to his own needs. He is always doing something for himself, and enjoys the exercise. The little egoist, even when he has "no language but a cry," uses that language to make known to the world that he wants something and wants it very much. As his wants increase, his exertions increase also. Arms and legs, fingers and toes, muscles and nerves and busy brain are all at work to get something which he desires. He is a mechanic fashioning his little world to his own uses. He is a despot who insists on his divine right to rule the subservient creatures around him. He is an inventor devising ways and means to secure all the ends which he has the wit to see. That these great works on which he has set his heart end in self is obvious enough, but we forgive him. Altruism will come in its own time.

In natural play a boy will be a horse or a driver. Either occupation gives him plenty to do. But the rôle of an elderly passenger, given a softly cushioned seat and deposited respectfully at the journey's end, he rejects with violent expressions of scorn. It is ignominious. He will be a policeman or robber or judge or executioner, just as the exigencies of the game demand. These are honorable positions worthy of one who belongs to the party of action. But do not impose upon him by asking him to act the part of

the respectable citizen who is robbed and who
does nothing but telephone for the police. He is
not fastidious and will take up almost anything
that is suggested, if it gives him the opportunity
of exerting himself. The demand for exertion is
the irreducible minimum.

Now to spoil all this fine enthusiasm you
must arrange everything in such a manner that
the eager little worker shall find everything
done before he has time to put his hand to it.
There must be no alluring possibilities in his
tiny universe. The days of creation, when "the
sons of God shouted for joy," must be passed
before he is ushered in. He must be presented
only with accomplished facts. There must be
nothing left for him to make or discover. He
must be told everything. All his designs must
be anticipated, by nurses and parents and teachers. They must give him whatever good things
they can think of before he has time to desire
them. From the time when elaborate mechanical
toys are put into his reluctant hands, it is understood that he is to be amused, and need not
amuse himself. His education is arranged for
him. His companions are chosen for him. There

is nothing for him to do, and if there were, there is no incentive for him to do it. In the game of life he is never allowed to be the horse. It is his fate to be the passenger.

A child is spoiled when he accepts the position into which fond, foolish parents thrust him. Being a passenger on what was presumably intended to be a pleasure excursion, he begins to find fault as soon as the journey becomes a little wearisome. He must find fault, because that is the only thing left for him to find. Having no opportunity to exercise his creative faculties, he becomes a petulant critic of a world he can neither enjoy nor understand. Taking for granted that everything should be done for him, he is angry because it is not done better. His ready-made world does not please him — why should it? It never occurs to him that if he does not like it he should try and make it better.

Unfortunately, the characteristics of the spoiled child do not vanish with childhood or even with adolescence. A university training does not necessarily transform petulance into ripe wisdom. Literary ability may only give fluent expression to a peevish spirit.

Among the innumerable children of an advanced civilization there are those who have been spoiled by the petting to which they have been subjected. Life has been made so easy for them that when they come upon hard places which demand sturdy endurance they break forth into angry complaints. They have been given the results of the complicated activities of mankind, without having done their share in the common tasks. They have not through personal endeavor learned how much everything costs. They are not able, therefore, to pay cheerfully for any future good. If it is not given to them at once they feel that they have a grievance. For friendly coöperation they are not prepared. They must have their own way or they will not play the game. Their fretful complaints are like those of the children in the old-time market-places: "We have piped unto you and you have not danced, we have mourned unto you and you have not lamented."

There is a fashionable attitude of mind among many who pride themselves on their acute intellectualism. It manifests itself in a supercilious compassion for the efforts and ambitions of the man of action. He, poor fellow, is well-meaning, but unilluminated. He is eager and energetic because he imagines that he is accomplishing something. If he were a serious thinker he would see that all effort is futile. We are here in an unintelligible world, a world of mighty forces, moving we know not whither. We are subject to passions and impulses which we cannot resist. We are never so helpless as when we are in the midst of human affairs. We have great words which we utter proudly. We talk of Civilization, Christianity, Democracy, and the like. What miserable failures they all are. Civilization has failed to produce contentment. It has failed to secure perfect justice between man and man, or to satisfy the hungry with bread. Christianity after all these centuries of preaching leaves mankind as we see it to-day — an armed camp, nation fighting nation, class warring against class. The democratic movement about which we hear so much is equally unsuccessful. After its brilliant promises it leaves us helpless against the passion and stupidity of the mob. Popular education adds to the tribulations of society. It rapidly increases the number of the discontented. The half-educated are led astray by quacks and demagogues who flourish mightily. The higher technical education increases that intellectual proletariat which Bismarck saw to be a peril. Science, which once was hailed as a deliverer, is now perceived to bring only the disillusioning knowledge of our limitations. The bankruptcy of Science follows closely upon the bankruptcy of Faith. Mechanical inventions, instead of decreasing the friction of life, enormously increase it. We are destined to be dragged along by our own machines which are to go faster and faster. Philanthropy increases the number of the unfit. The advances of medicine are only apparent, while statistics show that tuberculosis, a disease of early life, decreases, cancer and diseases of later life increase.

As for the general interest in social amelioration, that is the worst sign of all. " Coming events cast their shadows before," and we may see the shadow of the coming Revolution. Is there any symptom of decadence more sure than when the moral temperature suddenly rises above normal? Watch the clinical charts of Empire. In the period of national vigor the blood is cool. But the time arrives when the period of growth has passed. Then a boding sense comes on. The huge frame of the patient is feverish. The social conscience is sensitive. All sorts of soft-hearted proposals for helping the masses are proposed. The world rulers become too tender-hearted for their business. Then comes the end.

Read again the history of the Decline and Fall of the Roman Empire. How admirable were the efforts of the "good emperors," and how futile! Consider again the oft-repeated story of the way the humanitarianism of Rousseau ushered in the French Revolution and the Reign of Terror.

With such gloomy forebodings do the over-civilized thinkers and writers try to discourage the half-civilized and half-educated workers, who are trying to make things better. How shall we answer the prophets of ill?

Not by denying the existence of the evils they see, or the possibility of the calamities which they fear. What we object to is the mental attitude toward the facts that are discovered. The spoiled child, when it discovers something not to its liking, exaggerates the evil, and indulges its ill-temper.

The well-trained man faces the evil, studies it, measures it, and then sets to work. He is well aware that nothing human is perfect, and that to accomplish one thing is only to reveal another thing which needs to be done. There must be perpetual readjustment, and reconsideration. What was done yesterday must be done over again to-day in a somewhat different way. But all this does not prove the futility of effort. It only proves that the effort must be unceasing, and that it must be more and more wisely directed.

He compares, for example, Christianity as an ideal with Christianity as an actual achievement. He places in parallel columns the maxims of Jesus, and the policies of Christian nations and the actual state of Christian churches. The discrepancy is obvious enough. But it does not prove that Christianity is a failure; it only proves that its work is unfinished.

A political party may adopt a platform filled with excellent proposals which if thoroughly carried out would bring in the millennium. But it is too much to expect that it would all be accomplished in four years. At the end of that period we should not be surprised if the reformers should ask for a further extension of time.

The spoiled children of civilization eliminate from their problem the one element which is constant and significant—human effort. They forget that from the beginning human life has been a tremendous struggle against great odds. Nothing has come without labor, no advance has been without daring leadership. New fortunes have always had their hazards.

Forgetting all this, and accepting whatever comforts may have come to them as their right, they are depressed and discouraged by their vision of the future with its dangers and its difficulties. They habitually talk of the civilized world as on the brink of some great catastrophe which it is impossible to avoid. This gloomy foreboding is looked upon as an indication of wisdom.

It should be dismissed, I think, as an indication of childish unreason, unworthy of any one who faces realities. It is still true that "the morrow shall take thought for the things of itself. Sufficient unto the day is the evil thereof."

The notion that coming events cast shadows before is a superstition. How can they? A shadow must be the shadow of something. The only events that can cast a shadow are those which have already taken place. Behind them is the light of experience, shining upon actualities which intercept its rays.

The shadows which affright us are of our own making. They are projections into the future of our own experiences. They are sharply defined silhouettes, rather than vague omens. When we look at them closely we can recognize familiar features. We are dealing with cause and effect. What is done foreshadows what remains to be done. Every act implies some further acts as its results. When a principle is recognized its practical applications must follow. When men begin to reason from new premises they are bound to come to new conclusions.

It is evident that in the last half-century enough discoveries have been made to keep us busy for a long time. Every scientific advance upsets some custom and interferes with some vested interest. You cannot discover the truth about tuberculosis without causing a great deal of trouble to the owners of unsanitary dwellings. Some of them are widows whose little all is invested in this kind of property. The health inspectors make life more difficult for them.

Scholarly research among ancient manuscripts is the cause of destructive criticism. The scholar with the most peaceable intentions in the world disturbs some one's faith. His discovery perhaps involves the reconstruction of a whole system of philosophy.

A law is passed. The people are pleased with it, and then forget all about it. But by and by a conscientious executive comes into office who thinks it his duty to enforce the law. Such accidents are liable to happen in the most good-humored democracy. When he tries to enforce it there is a burst of angry surprise. He is treated as a revolutionist who is attacking the established order. And yet to the moderately philosophic observer the making of the law and its enforcement belong to the same process. The difficulty is that though united logically they are often widely separated chronologically.

The adjustment to a new theory involves changes in practice. But the practical man who has usually little interest in new theories is surprised and angry when the changes come. He looks upon them as arbitrary interferences with his rights.

Even when it is admitted that when considered in a large way the change is for the better, the question arises, Who is to pay for it? The discussion on this point is bound to be acrimonious, as we are not saints and nobody wants to pay more than his share of the costs of progress. Even the price of liberty is something which we grumble over.

You have noticed how it is when a new boulevard is laid in any part of the city. There is always a dispute between the municipality and the abutters. Should the abutters be assessed for betterments or should they sue for damages? Usually both actions are instituted. The cost of such litigation should be included in the price which the community pays for the improvement.

If people always knew what was good for them and acted accordingly, this would be a very different world, though not nearly so interesting. But we do not know what is good for us till we try; and human life is spent in a series of experiments. The experiments are costly, but there is no other way of getting results. All that we can say to a person who refuses to interest himself in these experiments, or who looks upon all experiments as futile which do not turn out as he wished, is that his attitude is childish. The great commandment to the worker or thinker is, — Thou shalt not sulk.

Sulking is no more admirable in those of great reputation than it is in the nursery. Thackeray declared that, in his opinion, " love is a higher intellectual exercise than hate." And looked at as an exercise of mental power courage must always be greater than the most highly intellectualized form of fear or despair.

I cannot take with perfect seriousness Matthew Arnold's oft-quoted lines:—

> " Achilles ponders in his tent,
> The kings of modern thought are dumb.
> Silent they are, though not content,
> And wait to see the future come.
> They have the grief men had of yore,
> But they contend and cry no more."

If that is ever the attitude of the best minds, it is only a momentary one of which they are

quickly ashamed. Achilles sulked in his tent
when he was pondering not a big problem, but
a small grievance. The kings of modern thought
who are described seem like kings out of a job.
We are inclined to turn from them to the intellectual monarchs *de facto*. They are the ones who
take up the hard job which the representatives of
the old régime give up as hopeless. For when
the king has abdicated and contends no more —
Long live the King!

The real thinkers of any age do not remain
long in a blue funk. They always find something important to think about. They always
point out something worth doing. They cannot
passively wait to see the future come. They are
too busy making it.

Matthew Arnold struck a truer note in Rugby
Chapel. The true leaders of mankind can never
be mere intellectualists. There must be a union
of intellectual and moral energy like that which
he recognized in his father. To the fainting, dis-
pirited race, —

> " Ye like angels appear,
>   Radiant with ardour divine,
>   Beacons of hope, ye appear !
>   Languor is not in your heart,

> Weakness is not in your word,
> Weariness not on your brow ;
> Ye alight in our van : at your voice
> Panic, despair, flee away."

When those whom we have looked upon as our intellectual leaders grow disheartened, we must remember that a lost leader does not necessarily mean a lost cause. When those whom we had called the kings of modern thought are dumb, we can find new leadership. " Change kings with us," replied an Irish officer after the panic of the Boyne ; "change kings with us, and we will fight you again."

ON REALISM AS AN INVESTMENT

❖❖❖❖

From a Real-Estate Dealer to a Realistic Novelist

DEAR SIR: —
    I have been for some time interested in your projects for the improvement of literature. When I saw your name in the newspapers, I looked you up in "Who's Who," and found that your rating is excellent. What pleased me was the bold way you attacked the old firms which have been living on their reputations. The way you showed up Dickens, Thackeray & Co. showed that you know a thing or two. As for W. Scott and the other speculators who have been preying on the credulity of the public, you gave them something to think about. You showed conclusively that instead of dealing in hard facts, they have been handing out fiction under the guise of novels.

Our minds run in the same channel: you deal in reality and I deal in realty, but the principle is the same. I inclose some of the literature which

I am sending out. You see, I warn people against investing in stocks and bonds. These are mere paper securities, which take to themselves wings and fly away. But if you can get hold of a few acres of dirt, there you are. When a panic comes along, and Wall Street goes to smash, you can sit on your front porch in South Canaan without a care. You have your little all in something real.

You followed the same line of argumentation. You showed that there was nothing imaginative about your work. You could give a warranty deed for every fact which you put on the market. I was so pleased with your method that I bought a job lot of your books, so that I could see for myself how you conducted your business. Will you allow me, as one in the same line, to indulge in a little criticism? I am afraid that you are making the same mistake I made when I first went into real estate. I was so possessed with the idea of the value of land that I became "land poor." It strikes me that a novelist may become reality poor in the same way; that is, by investing in a great many realities that are not worth what he pays for them.

You see, there is a fact which we do not mention in our circulars. There is a great deal of land lying out of doors. *Some* land is in great demand, and the real trick is to find out what that land is. You can't go out on the plains of Wyoming and give an acre of land the same value which an acre has in the Wall Street district. I speak from experience, having tried to convince the public that if the acres are real, the values I suggested must be real also. People would n't believe me, and I lost money.

And the same thing is true about improvements. They must be related to the market value of the land on which they are placed. A forty-story building at Goshenville Corners would be a mistake. There is no call for it.

This is the mistake which I fear you have been making. Your novel is a carefully prepared structure, and must have cost a great deal, but it is built on ground which is not worth enough to justify the investment. It has not what we call "site value." You yourself declare that you have no particular interest in the characters you describe at such length. All that you have to say for them is that they are real. It is as if I were to put up an expensive apartment-house on a vacant lot I have at North Ovid. North Ovid is real, and so would be the apartment-house; but what of it?

There are ninety millions of people in this country, all with characters which might be carefully studied, if we had time. But we have n't the time. So we have to choose our intimates. We prefer to know those who seem to us most worth knowing. You should remember that the novelist has no monopoly on realism. The newspapers are full of all sorts of realities. The historian is a keen competitor.

Do you know that when I went to the bookstore to get your works I fell in with a book on Garibaldi by a man named Trevelyan. When I got home I sat down with it and could n't let it go. Garibaldi was all the time doing things, which you never allow your characters to do because you think they would not be real. He was acting in the most romantic and heroic manner possible. And his Thousand trooped after him as gayly as if they were in a melodrama. And yet I understand that Garibaldi was a real person, and that his exploits can be authenticated.

The competition in your line of business is

fierce. You try to hold the reader's attention to the states of mind of a few futile persons who never did anything in particular that would make people want to know them exhaustively. And then along comes the historian who tells all about some one who does things they are interested in.

You can't wonder at the result. People who ought to be interested in fiction are carried away by biography, and the chances are that some of them will never come back. When they once get a taste for highly spiced intellectual victuals, you can't get them to relish the breakfast food you set before them. It seems to them insipid.

I know what you will say about Garibaldi. He was not your kind. You would n't touch such a character if it was offered to you at a bargain. After looking over that expedition to Sicily you would say that there was nothing in it for you. The motives were n't complicated enough. It was just plain heroics. You don't care so much for passions as for problems. You want something to analyze.

Well, what do you say to Cavour? When I was deep in Garibaldi I found I could n't understand what he was driving at without knowing something about Cavour who was always mixed up with what was going on in that section of the world.

So I took up a Life of Cavour by a man named Thayer. It's the way I have ; one thing suggests another. Once I went up to Duluth and invested in some corner lots on Superior Street. That suggested Superior City, just across the river. The two towns were running each other down at a great rate just then, so I stopped at West Superior to see what it had to say for itself. The upshot of the matter was that I sized up the situation about like this. A big city has *got* to grow up at the head of Lake Superior. If Duluth grows as much as it thinks it will, it's bound to take in Superior. And if Superior grows as much as it thinks it will, it can't help taking in Duluth. So I concluded that the best thing for me was to take a flier in both.

When I saw what a big proposition the Unification of Italy was, I knew that there was room for the development of some mighty interesting characters before they got through with the business. So I plunged into the Life of Cavour, and I've never regretted it.

Talk about problems! That hero of yours in your last book — I know you don't believe in heroes, — at any rate, the leading man — was an innocent child walking with his nurse along Easy Street, when compared with Cavour. Cavour had fifty problems at the same time, and all of them were insoluble to every one except himself.

His project, as I have just told you, was the unification of Italy. But he had n't any regulated monopoly in the business. A whole bunch of unifiers were ahead of him; each one of them was trying to unify Italy in his own way. They were all working at cross-purposes.

Now Cavour did n't try, as you might have expected, to reconcile these people. He saw that it could n't be done. He did n't mind their hating one another; when they got too peaceable he would make an occasion for them to hate him. He kept them all irreconcilably at work, till, in spite of themselves, they got to working together. And when they began to do that, Cavour would encourage them in it. As long as they were all working for Italy he did n't care what they thought of each other or of him. He had his eye on the main chance — for Italy.

I notice that in your novel, when your man got into trouble he threw up the sponge. That rather turned me against him and I wished I had n't wasted so much time on his affairs. That was n't the way with Thayer's hero. One of the largest deals Cavour ever made was with Napoleon III, who at that time had the reputation of being the biggest promoter of free institutions in Europe. He was a regular wizard in diplomacy. Whatever he said went. You see they had n't realized then that he was doing business on borrowed capital.

Well, Napoleon agreed to underwrite, for Cavour, the whole project of Italian Unity. Everybody thought it was going through all right, when suddenly Napoleon, from a place called Villafranca, wired that the deal was off.

That floored Cavour. He was down and out. He could n't realize ten cents on the dollar on his securities. If he had been like your man, Thayer would have had to bring his book to an end with that chapter. He would have left the reader plunged in gloom.

Cavour was mad for awhile and went up to Switzerland to cool off. Thayer describes the way he went up to a friend's house, near Lake Geneva, with his coat on his arm. "Unannounced, he strode into the drawing-room, threw himself into an easy-chair, and asked for a glass of iced water."

Then he poured out his wrath over the Villafranca incident, but he did n't waste much time over that. In a few moments he was enthusiastically telling of the new projects he had formed. "We must not look back, but forward," he told his friends. "We have followed one road. It is blocked. Very well, we will follow another."

That's the kind of man Cavour was. You forgot that he was a European statesman. When you saw him with his coat off, drinking ice-water and talking about the future, you felt toward him just as you would toward a first-rate American who was of Presidential size.

Now, I 'm not saying that there 's any more realism to the square inch in a Life of Cavour than in a Life of Napoleon III. It would take as much labor on the part of a biographer to tell what Napoleon III really was as to tell what Cavour really was — perhaps more. But you come up against the law of supply and demand. You can't get around that. There is n't much inquiry for Napoleon, now that his boom is over.

The way Thayer figured it was, I suppose, something like this. It would take eight or ten years to assemble the materials for a first-rate biography such as he wished to make. If he chose Napoleon there would be steady deterioration in the property, and when the improvements were put on there would be no demand. If he put the same work on Cavour, he would get the unearned increment. I think he showed his sense.

Of course the biographer has the advantage of you in one important particular. He knows how his story is coming out. In a way, he's betting on a certainty. Now you, as I judge, don't know how your story is coming out, and if it does n't come out, all you have to do is to say that is the way you meant it to be. You cut off so many square feet of reality, and let it go at that. Now that is very convenient for you, but from the reader's point of view, it's unsatisfactory. It mixes him up, and he feels a grudge against you whenever he thinks how much better he might have spent his time than in following a plot that came to nothing. You see you are running up against that same law of supply and demand. There are so many failures in the world that the market is overstocked with them. There is a demand for successes.

When I was in an old house which I took on the foreclosure of a mortgage the other day, I came upon a little old novel, of a hundred years ago. It was the sentimental kind that you despise. It was called "Alonzo and Melissa," which was enough to condemn it in your eyes. But the preface seemed to me to have some sense.

The author says : " It is believed that this story contains no indecorous stimulants, nor is it filled with inexplicated incidents imperceptible to the understanding. When anxieties have been excited by involved and doubtful events, they are afterwards elucidated by their consequences. In this the writer believes that he has generally copied Nature."

I have a feeling that those inexplicated incidents in your novel might have been elucidated by their consequences if you had chosen a person whose actions were of the kind to have some important consequences. In tying up to an inconsequential person you lost that chance.

I don't mean to discourage you, because I believe you have it in you to make a novel that would be as interesting as half the biographies that are written. But you must learn a trick from the successful biographers, and not invest in second-rate realities. The best is none too good. You have to exercise judgment in your initial investment.

Now, if I were going to build a realistic novel, and had as much skill in detail as you have, and as much intellectual capital to invest, I would go right down to the business centre, so to speak, and invest in a really valuable piece of reality; and then I would develop it. The first investment might seem pretty steep, but it would pay in the end. If you could get a big man, enthusiastic over a big cause, in conflict with big forces, and bring in a lot of worth-while people to back him up, and then bring the whole thing to some big conclusion, you would have a novel that would be as real as the biographies I have been reading, and as interesting. I think it would be worth trying.

Respectfully yours,

R. S. LANDMANN.

P. S. If you don't feel that you can afford to make such a heavy investment as I have suggested, why don't you put your material into a short story?

TO A CITIZEN OF THE OLD SCHOOL

◆◆◆◆

OUR talk last night set me to thinking. It was the first time during all the years of our acquaintance that I had ever heard you speak in a discouraged tone. You have always been healthy to a fault, and your good-humor has been contagious. Especially has it been pleasant to hear you talk about the country and its Manifest Destiny.

I remember, some years ago, how merrily you used to laugh about the "calamity-howler," whose habitat at that time was Kansas. The farmers of Kansas were not then as prosperous as they are now. When several bad years came together they did n't like it, and began to make complaints. Their raucous cries you found very amusing.

The calamity-howler, being ignorant of the laws of political economy and of the conditions of progress, did not take his calamities in the spirit in which they were offered to him by the rest of the country. He did not find satisfaction in the thought that other people were prosperous though he was not. Instead of acting reasonably and voting the straight ticket from motives of party loyalty, he raised all sorts of irrelevant issues. He treated Prosperity as if it were a local issue, instead of a plank in the National Platform.

Now, all this was opposed to your good-natured philosophy of progress. You were eminently practical, and it was a part of your creed never to "go behind the returns." As to Prosperity, it was "first come, first served." In this land of opportunity the person who first sees an opportunity should take it, asking no questions as to why he came by it. It is his by right of discovery.

You were always a great believer in the good old American doctrine of Manifest Destiny. This was a big country and destined to grow bigger. To you bigness was its own excuse for being. Optimism was as natural as breathing. It was manifest destiny that cities and corporations and locomotives and armies and navies and national debts and daily newspapers, with their Sunday supplements, and bank clearances and tariffs and insurance companies and the price of living should go up. It was all according to a beautiful natural law, "as fire ascending seeks the sun." Besides these things, it was manifest destiny that other things not so good should grow bigger also, — graft and slums and foolish luxury. They were all involved in the increasing bigness of things.

Sometimes you would grumble about them, but in a good-natured way, as one who recognized their inevitability. Just as you said, boys will be boys, so you said, politicians will be politicians, and business is business. If one is living in a growing country he must not begrudge the cost of the incidentals.

In your talk there was a cheerful cynicism which amazed the slower-witted foreigner. You talked of the pickings and stealings of your elected officers as you would of the pranks of a precocious youngster. It was all a part of the day's growth. Yet you were really public-spirited. You would have sprung to arms in a moment if you had thought that your country was in danger or that its institutions were being undermined.

Your good-natured tolerance was a part of

your philosophy of life. It was bound up in your triumphant Americanism. You were a hero-worshipper, and you delighted in "big men." The big men who gained the prizes were efficient and unscrupulous and unassuming; that is, they never assumed to be better than their neighbors. They looked ahead, they saw how things were going, and went with them. And on the whole, things, you believed, were going well. Though they were not scrupulously just, these big men were generous, and were willing to give away what they had acquired. Though grasping, they were not avaricious. They grasped things with the strong prehensile grasp of the infant, rather than with the clutch of the miser. They took them because they were there, and not because they had any well-defined idea as to whether they belonged to them or not.

These big men were very likable. They were engrossed in big projects, and they were doing necessary work in the development of the country. They naturally took the easiest and most direct methods to get at results. They would not go out of the way to corrupt a legislature any more than they would go out of the way to find a range of mountains. But if the mountain stood in the way of the railroad, they would go through it regardless of expense. If the legislature was in their way, they would deal with it as best they could. They were willing to pay what it cost to accomplish a purpose which they believed was good.

Their attitude toward the Public was one which you did not criticize, for it seemed to you to be reasonable. The Public was an abstraction, like Nature. We are all under the laws of Nature. But Nature does n't mind whether we consciously obey or not. She goes her way, and we go ours. We get all she will let us have. So with the Public. The Public was not regarded as a person or as an aggregate of persons, it was the potentiality of wealth. They never thought of the Public as being starved or stunted, or even as being seriously inconvenienced because of what they took from it, any more than they thought of Nature being the poorer because of the electricity which they induced to run along their wires. A public franchise was a plum growing on a convenient tree. A wise man would wait till it was ripe and then, when no one was looking, would pick it for himself. The whole transaction was a trial of wits between rival pickers. A special privilege, according to this view, involved no special obligations; it was a reward for special abilities. Once given, it was property to be enjoyed in perpetuity.

This was the code of ethics which you, in common with multitudes of American citizens, accepted. You have yourself prospered. Indeed, things had gone so well with you in this best of all countries that any fundamental change seemed unthinkable.

But that a change has come seems evident from your conversation last night. All that fine optimism which your friends have admired seemed to have deserted you. There was a querulous note which was strangely out of keeping with your usual disposition. It was what you have been accustomed to stigmatize as un-American. When you discussed the present state of the country, you talked — you will pardon me for saying it — for all the world like a calamity-howler.

The country, you said, is in a bad way, and it must be awakened from its lethargy. After a period of unexampled prosperity and marvelous development, something has happened. Just what it is you don't really know, but it's very alarming. Instead of working together for Prosperity, the people are listening to demagogues, and trying all sorts of experiments, half of which you are sure are unconstitutional. The captains of industry who have made this the biggest country in the world are thwarted in their plans for further expansion.

There are people who are criticizing the courts, and there are courts which are criticizing business enterprises that they don't understand. There are so-called experts — mere college professors — who are tinkering the tariff. There are over-zealous executives who are currying favor with the crowd by enforcing laws which are well enough on the statute books, but which were never meant to go further. As if matters were not bad enough already, there are demagogues who are stirring up class feeling by proposing new laws. Party loyalty is being undermined, and the new generation does n't half understand the great issues which have been settled for all time. It is rashly interested in new issues. For the life of you, you say, you can't understand what these issues are.

New and divisive questions which lead only to faction are propounded so that the voters are confused. The great principle of Representative Government, on which the Republic was founded, is being attacked. Instead of choosing experienced men to direct public policy, there is an appeal to the passions of the mob. The result of all this agitation is an unsettlement that paralyzes business. The United States is in danger of losing the race for commercial supremacy. Germany will forge ahead of us. Japan will catch us. Socialism and the Yellow Peril will be upon us. The Man on Horseback will appear, and what shall we do then?

I did not understand whether you looked for these perils to come together, or whether they were to appear in orderly succession. But I came to the conclusion that either the country is in a bad way, or you are. You will pardon me if I choose the latter alternative, for I too am an optimistic American, and I like to choose the lesser of two evils. If there is an attack of " hysteria," I should like to think of it as somewhat localized, rather than having suddenly attacked the whole country.

Now, my opinion is that the American people were never minding their own business more good-humoredly and imperturbably than at the present moment. They have been slowly and silently making up their minds, and now they are beginning to express a deliberate judgment. What you take to be the noise of demagogues, I consider to be the sober sense of a great people which is just finding adequate expression.

You seem to be afraid of an impending revolution, and picture it as a sort of French Revolution, a destructive overturn of all existing institutions. But may not the revolution which we are passing through be something different, — a great American revolution, which is being carried through in the characteristic American fashion?

Walt Whitman expresses the great characteristic of American history: "Here is what moves in magnificent masses careless of particulars."

It is this mass movement, slow at first, but swift and irresistible when the mass has come to consciousness of its own tendency, which has always confounded astute persons who have been interested only in particulars. It is a movement like that of the Mississippi at flood-time. The great river flows within its banks as long as it can. But the time comes when the barriers are too frail to hold back the mighty waters. Then the river makes, very quickly, a channel for itself. You cannot understand what has happened till you take into account the magnitude of the river itself.

Now, the successful man of affairs, who has been intent on the incidents of the passing day, is often strangely oblivious of the mass movements. You, for example, are disturbed by the unrest which is manifest, and you look for some one whom you can blame for the disturbance. But perhaps no one is to blame.

I think that what is happening may be traced to a sufficient cause. We are approaching the end of one great era in American history and we are preparing, as best we may, for a new era. The consciousness of the magnitude of the change has come to us rather suddenly. One big job which has absorbed the energies and stimulated the ambition of Americans for three hundred years is practically finished. Some work still remains to be done on it, but it no longer demands the highest ability. The end is in sight.

This work has been the settlement of a vast territory, lying between the Atlantic and Pacific, with a population of white men. It was a task so big in itself that it fired the imagination and developed that peculiar type of character which we call American. In its outlines the task was so broad and simple that it could be comprehended by the most ordinary intelligence. It was so inevitable that it impressed upon all those engaged in it the belief in Manifest Destiny.

What has been treated by incompetent critics as mere boastfulness has in reality been practical sagacity and foresight. Sam Slick was only expressing a truth when he said, "The Yankees see further than most folks." This was not because of any innate cleverness but because of their advantage in position. Americans have had a more unobstructed view of the future than had the people of the overcrowded Old World. The settlers on the shores of the Atlantic had behind them a region which belonged to them and their children. They soon became aware of the riches of this hinterland and of its meaning for the future. This vast region must be settled. Roads must be built over the mountains, the forests must be felled, mines must be opened up, farms must be brought under the plow, great cities must be built by the rivers and lakes, there must be schools and churches and markets established where now the tribes of Indians roam. The surplus millions of Europe must be transported to this wilderness.

It was a big task and yet a simple one. The movement was as obvious as that of Niagara — Niagara is wonderful but inevitable. A great deal of water flowing over a great deal of rock, that is all there is of it. The destiny of America was equally obvious from the beginning, Here was a great deal of land which was destined to be inhabited by a great many people. It didn't matter very much what kind of people they were so that they were healthy and industrious. The greatness of the country was assured if only there were enough of them.

From the very first the future greatness of the land was seen by open-eyed explorers. They all were able to appreciate it. Captain John Smith does not compare Virginia with Great Britain; he compares it to the whole of Europe. After mentioning the natural resources of each country, he

declares that the new land had all these and
more, and needed only men to develop them.
And Captain John Smith's forecast has proved
to be correct.

In the first half of the last century, a party of
twenty young men from Cambridge, Massachusetts, started on what at that time was a great
adventure, the overland journey to Oregon. The
preface to Wyeth's " Oregon Expedition" throws
light on the ideas of those who were not states-
men or captains of industry, but only plain
American citizens sharing the vision which was
common.

" The spot where our adventurer was born and
grew up had many peculiar and desirable advantages over most others in the County of Middle-
sex. Besides rich pasturage, numerous dairies,
and profitable orchards, it possessed the luxuries
of well-cultivated gardens of all sorts of culinary
vegetables, and all within three miles of Boston
Market House, and two miles of the largest live-
cattle market in New England." Besides these
blessings there is enumerated "a body of water
commonly called Fresh Pond."

" But Mr. Wyeth said, ' All this availeth me

nothing, so long as I read books in which I find that by going only about four thousand miles overland, from the shore of our Atlantic to the shore of the Pacific, after we have there entrapped and killed the beavers and otters, we shall be able, after building vessels for the purpose, to carry our most valuable peltry to China and Cochin China, our sealskins to Japan, and our superfluous grain to various Asiatic ports, and lumber to the Spanish settlements on the Pacific; and to become rich by underworking and underselling the people of Hindustan; and, to crown all, to extend far and wide the traffic in oil, by killing tame whales on the spot, instead of sailing around the stormy region of Cape Horn.'

"All these advantages and more were suggested to divers discontented and impatient young men. Talk to them of the great labor, toil, risk, and they would turn a deaf ear to you; argue with them and you might as well reason with a snow-storm."

If you would understand the driving power of America, you must understand "the divers discontented and impatient young men" who in each generation have found in the American wilderness an outlet for their energies. In the rough contacts with untamed Nature they learned to be resourceful. Emerson declared that the country went on most satisfactorily, not when it was in the hands of the respectable Whigs, but when in the hands of " these rough riders — legislators in shirt-sleeves — Hoosier, Sucker, Wolverine, Badger — or whatever hard-head Arkansas, Oregon, or Utah sends, half-orator, half-assassin, to represent its wrath and cupidity at Washington."

The men who made America had an " excess of virility." " Men of this surcharge of arterial blood cannot live on nuts, herb-tea, and elegies; cannot read novels and play whist; cannot satisfy all their wants at the Thursday Lecture and the Boston Athenæum. They pine for adventure and must go to Pike's Peak; had rather die by the hatchet of the Pawnee than sit all day and every day at the counting-room desk. They are made for war, for the sea, for mining, hunting, and clearing, and the joy of eventful living."

In Emerson's day there was ample scope for all these varied energies on the frontier. " There are Oregons, Californias, and Exploring Expeditions enough appertaining to America to find them in files to gnaw and crocodiles to eat."

But it must have occurred to some one to ask, "What will happen when the Oregons and Californias are filled up?" Well, the answer is, "See what is happening now." Instead of settling down to herb-tea and elegies, Young America, having finished one big job, is looking for another. The noises which disturb you are not the cries of an angry proletariat, but are the shouts of eager young fellows who are finding new opportunities. They have the same desire to do big things, the same joy in eventful living, that you had thirty years ago. Only the tasks that challenge them have taken a different form.

When you hear the words "Conservation," "Social Service," "Social Justice," and the like, you are apt to dismiss them as mere fads. You think of the catchwords of ineffective reformers whom you have known from your youth. But the fact is that they represent to-day the enthusiasms of a new generation. They are big things, with big men behind them. They represent the Oregons and Californias toward which sturdy pioneers are moving, undeterred by obstacles.

The live questions to-day concern not the material so much as the moral development of the nation. For it is seen that the future welfare of the people depends on the creation of a finer type of civic life. Is this still to be a land of opportunity? Ninety millions of people are already here. What shall be done with the next ninety millions? That wealth is to increase goes without saying. But how is it to be distributed? Are we tending to a Plutocracy, or can a real Democracy hold its own? Powerful machinery has been invented. How can this machinery be controlled and used for truly human ends? We have learned the economies that result from organization. Who is to get the benefit of these economies?

So long as such questions were merely academic, practical persons like yourself paid little attention to them. Now they are being asked by persons as practical as yourself who are intent on 'getting results.' And what is more, they employ the instruments of precision furnished by modern science.

You have been pleased over the millions of dollars which have been lavished on education.

The fruits of this are now being seen. Hosts of able young men have been studying Government and Sociology and Economics and History. These have been the most popular courses in all our colleges. And they have been studied in a new way. The old formulas and the old methods have been fearlessly criticized. New standards of efficiency have been presented. The scientific method has been extended to the sphere of moral relations. It has been demonstrated to these young men that the resources of the country may be indefinitely increased by the continuous application of trained intelligence to definite ends. The old Malthusian doctrine has given way before applied science. The population may be doubled and the standard of living increased at the same time, if we plan intelligently. The expert can serve the public as efficiently as he has served private interests, if only the public can be educated to appreciate him, and persuaded to employ him.

This is what the "social unrest" means in America. It is not the unrest of the weak and the unsuccessful. It is the unrest of the strong and ambitious. You cannot still it by talking about prosperity: of course we are prosperous, after a fashion, but it is a fashion that no longer pleases us. We want something better and we propose to get it. What disturbs you is the appearance in force of a generation that has turned its attention to a new set of problems, and is attempting to solve them by scientific methods. It is believed that there is a Science of Government as well as an Art of Politics. The new generation has a respect, born of experience, for the expert. It seeks the man who knows rather than the clever manager. It demands of public servants not simply that they be honest, but that they be efficient.

Its attitude to the political boss is decidedly less respectful than that to which you were accustomed. You looked upon him as a remarkably astute character, and you attributed to him an uncanny ability to forecast the future. These young men have discovered that his ability is only a vulgar error. Remove the conditions created by public indifference and ignorance, and he vanishes. In restoring power to the people, they find that a hundred useful things can be done which the political wiseacres declared to be impossible.

When I consider the new and vigorous forces in American life I cannot agree with your apprehensions; but there is one thing which you said with which I heartily agree. You said that you wished we might settle down to sound and constructive work, and get rid of the "muck-raker."

I agree with you that the muck-raker stands in the way of large plans for betterment. But it might be well to refresh our minds in regard to what is really meant by the man with the muck-rake. He is not the man who draws our attention to abuses which can be abolished by determined effort. He is the man who apologizes for abuses that are profitable to himself. He prefers his petty interests to any ideal good. His character was most admirably drawn by Bunyan:—

"The Interpreter takes them apart again, and has them first into a room where was a man that could look no way but downwards, with a muck-rake in his hand. There stood also one over his head with a celestial crown in His hand, and proffered him that crown for his muck-rake, but the man did neither look up nor regard, but raked to himself the straws, the small sticks, and the dust of the floor.

"'Then,' said Christiana, 'I persuade myself that I know somewhat the meaning of this; for this is the figure of a man of this world, is it not, good sir?'

"'Thou hast said right,' said he. . . .

"'Then,' said Christiana, 'O deliver me from this muck-rake.'

"'That prayer,' said the Interpreter, 'has lain by till it is almost rusty. "Give me not riches," is scarce the prayer of one in ten thousand.'"

The man with the muck-rake, then, is one who can look no way but downward, and is so intent on collecting riches for himself that he does not see or regard any higher interests. I agree with you that if we are to have any constructive work in American society the first thing is to get rid of the man with the muck-rake, and to put in his place the Man with a Vision.

THE END

𝕮𝖍𝖊 𝕽𝖎𝖛𝖊𝖗𝖘𝖎𝖉𝖊 𝕻𝖗𝖊𝖘𝖘

CAMBRIDGE . MASSACHUSETTS

U . S . A

PEOPLE OF POPHAM

By MARY C. E. WEMYSS

"As vivid in its way as 'Cranford.'" — *Boston Transcript*.

"One of the most charming chronicles of village life ever written." — *Living Age*.

"Such a book as this may be read aloud evening after evening, with recurrent zest, with enjoyment of its humor, its quaint and human personages as they take their unhurried way through agreeable pages." — *Louisville Courier Journal*.

"A book which will give many readers a rare pleasure." — *Chicago Evening Post*.

"A sort of modern 'Cranford,' good to read all the way through." — *Minneapolis Journal*.

Illustrated. $1.20 *net*. Postage 11 cents.

HOUGHTON
MIFFLIN
COMPANY

BOSTON
AND
NEW YORK

A YEAR IN A COAL-MINE

By JOSEPH HUSBAND

"Mr. Husband enables the reader to carry away a vitalized impression of a coal-mine, its working and its workers, and a grasp of vivid details." — *San Francisco Chronicle*.

"It is a story of vivid and compelling interest and every word bears the impress of truth." — *Living Age*.

"Apart from its informative value, this is a book that no one can fail to enjoy." — *Philadelphia Press*.

"A refreshingly frank narrative." — *New York Sun*.

With frontispiece. $1.10 *net*. Postage 9 cents.

HOUGHTON
MIFFLIN
COMPANY

BOSTON
AND
NEW YORK

ROUTINE AND IDEALS

By Le Baron R. Briggs, *President of Rad-cliffe College.*

16mo, $1.00, *net.* Postage 9 cents.

"Common sense enriched by culture describes everything which Dean, or, as he ought now to be called, President, Briggs says or writes. The genius of sanity, sound judgment, and high aim seems to preside over his thought, and he combines in an unusual degree the faculty of vision and the power of dealing with real things in a real way." — *The Outlook*, New York.

SCHOOL, COLLEGE, AND CHARACTER

By the Author of " Routine and Ideals."

16mo, $1.00, *net.* Postage 8 cents.

"With the soundest good sense and with frequent humorous flashes, Dean Briggs takes students and parents into his confidence, and shows them the solution of college problems from the point of view, not of the 'office' but of a very clear-thinking, whole-souled man *in* the 'office'" — *The World's Work*, New York.

Houghton Mifflin Company, Publishers

BOSTON AND NEW YORK

JOHN PERCYFIELD

By C. HANFORD HENDERSON

Crown 8vo, gilt top, $1.50

HOUGHTON
MIFFLIN
COMPANY

TOUT
OU
BIEN
RIEN

BOSTON
AND
NEW YORK